PASS THE
U.S. CITIZENSHIP
EXAM

PASS THE U.S. CITIZENSHIP EXAM ▶

Fifth Edition

LEARNINGEXPRESS®

NEW YORK

All rights reserved under International and Pan American Copyright Conventions.
Published in the United States by LearningExpress, New York.

Cataloging-in-Publication Data is on file with the Library of Congress.

ISBN 978-1-61103-096-9

Printed in the United States of America

9 8 7 6 5 4 3   18 19 20 21 22

Fifth Edition

For more information on LearningExpress, other LearningExpress products, or bulk sales,
please write to us at:
    224 W. 29th Street
    3rd Floor
    New York, NY 10001

CONTENTS

HOW TO USE THIS BOOK ▶

This book is designed to help you pass the United States Citizenship Exam. It also explains the process of how to become a United States citizen. However, this book does not give legal advice. Go to your lawyer for help with immigration laws. You may want to study this book by yourself, with a partner, or in a formal classroom. The book is written for people whose first language is not English.

What You Will Find in This Book

There are three sections in this book. Section I—Chapters 1, 2, and 3—gives you a complete overview of the process of becoming a U.S. citizen. Chapter 1 offers information about the benefits and responsibilities that come with U.S. citizenship. You should know why you want to become a U.S. citizen. Chapter 2 explains what you need to do to become a U.S. citizen. Remember that naturalization laws can change. Ask your lawyer or someone from the U.S. Citizenship and Immigration Services (USCIS) for updated information. Chapter 3 shows you which USCIS regional office you should contact for more information or to send your completed N-400 application form.

Section II of this book—Chapters 4, 5, 6, and 7—cover the exam, each with vocabulary words, relevant questions, and exercises. By the end of this section, you will have seen the entire list of 100 civics questions, as well as all vocabulary words for the reading and writing portion of the exam. After you study all the concepts, do the exercises at the end of each lesson. You will find the answers to the exercises and review tests at the end of Section II. Do not look at the answers until after you try to answer each question.

Section III—Chapters 8, 9, and 10—will walk you through the steps of the actual citizenship interview. Each chapter covers a different stage of the interview process. Chapter 8 prepares you for the small talk, the truth oath, and the identity check. Chapter 9 helps familiarize you with the information on your N-400 form and discusses how your interviewer may ask you questions about your information. Chapter 10 goes over the questions that the interviewer may ask you on basic U.S. history, civics, reading, and writing from the questions covered in Section II. Work slowly and carefully through each lesson, and practice all the exercises. The review at the end of Section III revisits some of the key concepts.

The appendix includes a sample copy of the N-400 Application for Naturalization for you to practice filling out. You will also find a list of useful websites and books to use as resources.

After reading and studying this book, you will be well on your way to passing the U.S. Citizenship Exam. Good luck!

STUDY FOR SUCCESS!

You will have the most success with this book if you:

- find a quiet place to work
- make sure you have good lights
- turn off the T.V. and computer
- avoid all other distractions
- create a study group with others who are taking the test

Set realistic study goals and a realistic schedule—and stick to them!

SECTION

I ▶ PROCESS OVERVIEW

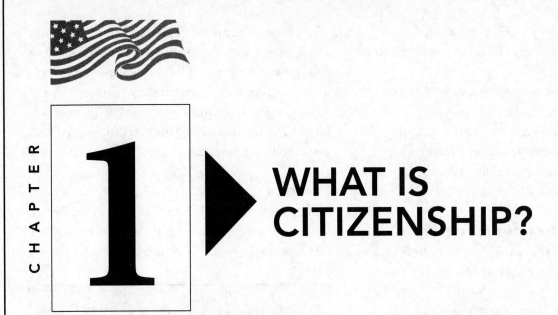

1 ▶ WHAT IS CITIZENSHIP?

Since its founding over 200 years ago, America has stood for the ideals of democracy, independence, and freedom. Every year, hundreds of thousands of people come to America seeking new opportunities in this "land of the free" and "home of the brave." Many of these immigrants take the final step in making America their new home by becoming U.S. citizens. Do you want to take this step? Before you decide to become an American citizen, you should be aware of the benefits and responsibilities of citizenship.

Benefits of Citizenship

- You get the right to vote in elections.
- You get to run for certain public offices.
- You are eligible for more jobs with the federal and state governments.
- Your immediate family members living abroad have priority in coming to live in the U.S. permanently.
- Your children born abroad, after you become a citizen, may be eligible for automatic U.S. citizenship.
- Your unmarried children, under the age of 18, are eligible for automatic U.S. citizenship.
- You may be eligible for some Social Security benefits even if you live in another country.
- You may live outside the U.S. without losing your citizenship.

- You get to travel with a U.S. passport.
- You get to reenter the U.S. more easily, when traveling abroad.
- You do not have to renew your green card or report a change of address.
- You get more government benefits including ongoing Supplemental Security Income.
- You may not be deported for crimes committed *after* you become a U.S. citizen.

Responsibilities of Citizenship

- You must take an Oath of Allegiance to the U.S.
- You must give up allegiance to other nations/sovereignties.
- You must serve the country, when required by law.
- You may participate in government by voting in elections.
- You must serve on a jury, when asked.

However, the most important reason to become a U.S. citizen is if you identify with American ideals and you love America. This book will give you a basic understanding of U.S. civics, history, basic reading and writing skills, and a review of the USCIS interview format, so that you can pass the U.S. Citizenship Exam and become an American citizen.

Practice

Think about the reasons why you want to become an American citizen, because you may need to answer this question in your USCIS interview:

> Why do you want to become a United States citizen?

2 ▶ THE PROCESS OF BECOMING A CITIZEN

This chapter will show you how you can become a U.S. citizen. There are many steps to this process and it will take several months to complete all the steps. The best way to prepare for the process of becoming a citizen is to know what to expect. Read this chapter carefully. See the flowchart on the following page for an overview of the process.

Citizenship Process

The process usually takes an average of six to nine months, according to USCIS. Be sure to submit all the correct documents that USCIS requests.

Eligibility Quiz

Find out if you are ready to apply for U.S. citizenship. Circle either **Yes** or **No**.

Yes No Are you at least 18 years old?

Yes No Have you been a lawful permanent resident of the United States either for five years, OR for three years if you have been married for three years to a person who has been a U.S. citizen for at least three years?

Yes No During the past five years, have you been physically present in the United States for at least $2\frac{1}{2}$ years (30 months), OR $1\frac{1}{2}$ years (18 months) if you are married to a U.S. citizen?

Yes No Have you lived within the state or district in which you currently reside for at least three months?

Yes No Do you have good moral character?

Yes No Can you read, write, and speak simple English?

Yes No Do you know about U.S. government and history?

Yes No Are you willing to swear loyalty to the United States?

If you circled **Yes** to all of the questions, you are ready to apply to become a U.S. citizen. If you answered **No** to any of the questions, ask an immigration specialist if you are ready. There are special reasons for answering **No**, and you may still be able to apply to become a U.S. citizen.

The Application

You need to submit an application called the N-400 Application for Naturalization to the USCIS. You also have to submit two photographs of yourself and a money order, personal check, or cashier's check for the application and fingerprint fee (when this book was made, the application fee was $595 plus an $85 fingerprint fee). The fees may be paid in one check (total of the check is $680). Applicants 75 years of age or older are not charged a finger print fee. Their total fee is $595. Make the check payable to the U.S. Citizenship and Immigration Services.

SEND THESE TO THE USCIS

- Form N-400
- Two photographs
- One check for the total fee, made payable to U.S. Citizenship and Immigration Services

You can get the N-400 application from a USCIS office near you. Visit the USCIS website at www.uscis.gov or call 1-800-375-5283 to find your local USCIS office. Then you can do one of the following:

- Write them a letter to ask for the form.
- Go to the office and pick up the form.
- Call them on the phone and ask for the form.
- Download and print the forms at www.uscis.gov.

Tell the truth when you fill out the N-400 application form. Get help if you need it. See Chapter 3 for where to find help.

TIPS FOR ASSEMBLING YOUR APPLICATION

- Print clearly with black ink or type your answers.
- Check your application for spelling errors.
- Check your application to be sure that you have completed all of the items on the form.
- Before inserting your application into a mailing envelope, make copies of every page for your records.
- Gather all necessary supporting documents and include copies.
- Keep all copies and material in a safe place, for future reference.
- Follow the instructions for submitting payment—do not send cash.
- Clearly mark both the envelope and your cover letter with the form type: *N-400 Application for Naturalization.*
- Use the correct mailing address.

Fingerprints

Do not send a fingerprint card with your N-400 application. After the USCIS receives your N-400 application, they will send you an appointment letter with the address of the nearest USCIS-authorized fingerprint site. Read the instructions in the appointment letter. Take the letter to the USCIS-authorized fingerprint site when you go to your fingerprint appointment. After you get your fingerprints taken, mail any additional documents that the USCIS might request and wait for them to schedule your interview.

Study

Read and study this book and any other material that will help you understand U.S. government and his-

tory. You need to know the material included in this book. You may also want to take a class on how to pass the U.S. Citizenship Exam.

The Test

The USCIS will test you about U.S. government and history during your interview. They will ask you questions in English and you will answer them out loud in English. During the interview, you will also need to write down one or two sentences that you hear. To pass the test, you must answer 60% of the questions correctly. If you do not pass the test, you will get one more try. If you do not pass the test the second time, you will have to start the whole process over and wait another several months to get a new interview date.

THREE IMPORTANT EXCEPTIONS

You can take the test in your native language (not English) if you are:
- Fifty-five (55) years old and have lived in America for 15 years as a lawful permanent resident

OR
- Fifty (50) years old and have lived in America for 20 years as a lawful permanent resident

You can take an easier test in your native language if you are:
- Sixty-five (65) years old and have lived in America for 20 years as a lawful permanent resident

These exceptions allow you to avoid the English writing and reading portion of the exam. You will still be required to answer civics questions in your native language, and answer application questions in your native language.

The Interview

You will be given a date to go for your USCIS interview. It may take 10–12 months to get a date for the interview. Be sure to attend your interview on the date you are given. If you must miss your interview, you should contact the office where your interview is scheduled as soon as possible, asking to reschedule your interview. At the interview, you must promise to tell the truth by taking an oath. You will be asked questions about your N-400 application. You will also be asked questions about yourself, your children, your work, and your life. You must answer these questions in English. If you have a physical, mental, or developmental disability, talk to an immigration specialist to find out if you can avoid speaking English and answering questions about the American government during the interview.

Swearing-In Ceremony

If you pass the test and the interview, you will get a letter within two months. The letter will tell you the date and time of a swearing-in ceremony. At the ceremony, you will take the Oath of Allegiance (say that you are loyal to the United States) and exchange your permanent residency card for a U.S. citizenship certificate. After the ceremony, you will be an American citizen.

The USCIS office may also continue your case. If your case is continued, it will add time to your naturalization process. The most common reasons for continuation are (1) failing the English and civics tests and/or (2) failing to give the USCIS the needed documents. If your case is continued, you will be asked to either come to a second interview or to provide additional documents. If you do not do what the USCIS requires, your application may be denied. If your application is denied, you will receive a written notice telling you why. If you feel that you have been wrongly denied citizenship, you may request a hearing with a USCIS officer. Your denial letter will explain how to request a hearing and will include the form you need.

3 ▶ HOW AND WHERE TO GET HELP

You can find help in becoming a U.S. citizen in many places. This chapter includes contact information for the USCIS lockbox facilities so you can find the one for your state. Other groups offer help too, and this chapter includes information on how to access that help.

USCIS Lockbox Facilities

Here is a list of where to send your completed N-400 Application for Naturalization form. There are two regional USCIS lockbox facilities. Look for your state and then send your N-400 application to the address that appears after your state.

Be sure to keep a copy of everything you send to USCIS.

If you live in one of these states:

Alaska	Kansas	Oregon
Arizona	Michigan	South Dakota
California	Minnesota	Utah
Colorado	Missouri	Washington
Hawaii	Montana	Wisconsin
Idaho	Nebraska	Wyoming
Illinois	Nevada	OR
Indiana	North Dakota	Territory of Guam
Iowa	Ohio	Commonwealth of the Northern Mariana Islands

Then send your completed N-400 application form to this address:

USCIS
P.O. Box 21251
Phoenix, AZ 85036

If you live in one of these states:

Alabama	Massachusetts	South Carolina
Arkansas	Mississippi	Tennessee
Connecticut	New Hampshire	Texas
Delaware	New Jersey	Vermont
Florida	New Mexico	Virginia
Georgia	New York	Washington, D.C.
Kentucky	North Carolina	West Virginia
Louisiana	Oklahoma	OR
Maine	Pennsylvania	Commonwealth of Puerto Rico
Maryland	Rhode Island	U.S. Virgin Islands

Then send your completed N-400 application form to this address:

USCIS
P.O. Box 660060
Dallas, TX 75266

USCIS Service Center for Military Members and Spouses

If you are filing an application under military provisions, then send your completed N-400 application to this address (regardless of where you live and whether you are filing from within the U.S. or abroad):

Nebraska Service Center
P.O. Box 87426
Lincoln, NE 68501-7426

USCIS Help

USCIS offers a customer service phone line to assist you during the naturalization process. To access this service, call 1-800-375-5283. There is no fee for the USCIS customer service.

Legal Help

You may want to pay for an attorney to help you complete the N-400 Application for Naturalization form. If so, look in your phone book for the phone number of your state's bar association or the Legal Aid Society. Many immigration attorneys also advertise in the yellow pages of the phone book. Be careful when you choose an attorney. Ask friends or relatives to suggest an attorney if they know of a good one.

One place you can contact for more information is the American Immigration Lawyers Association (AILA). It has over 10,000 attorneys who practice immigration law. AILA Member attorneys represent tens of thousands of U.S. families who have applied for permanent residence for their spouses, children, and other close relatives to lawfully enter and reside in the United States. You can ask for a referral to an immigration attorney by contacting them at:

American Immigration Lawyers Association
918 F Street, NW
Washington, D.C. 20004-1400
202-216-2400
www.ailalawyer.com

Community-Based Resources

Many local libraries and state governments offer free courses that help qualified candidates through the entire naturalization process, including preparation for the U.S. Citizenship Exam. Check with your local library and government to see what they offer. In addition, there are many national and community-based organizations that assist candidates with everything from exam preparation to legal services for free or low cost. Ask your local librarian to assist you with finding these organizations. You can also search the Internet using the following search terms alone or in combination, including your home state or city: *naturalization assistance*, *citizenship assistance*, *naturalization programs*, and *citizenship programs*.

II ▶ THE 100 QUESTIONS AND ENGLISH COMPREHENSION

The next four chapters will help you prepare for the exam, using the LearningExpress Test Preparation System and reviewing the U.S. civics, history, and government concepts that you may be tested on at your citizenship interview. Chapters 5, 6, and 7 cover several lessons, with vocabulary words, relevant questions, and exercises. Work slowly and carefully through each lesson, and complete all the exercises. The section review at the end of the section revisits some of these key concepts. At the end of this section, you'll find the official list of 100 questions and the official vocabulary word list. This covers three out of four parts of the citizenship exam. Study these questions and vocabulary words and you will be very prepared for the test. The answers to the exercises can be found starting on page 96.

Here's an outline of what's in this section:

THE LEARNINGEXPRESS TEST PREPARATION SYSTEM

CHAPTER OVERVIEW

Taking any exam can be tough. It demands a lot of preparation if you want to pass the U.S. Citizenship Exam. The LearningExpress Test Preparation System, developed exclusively for LearningExpress by leading test experts, gives you the discipline and attitude you need to achieve your dream of becoming a U.S. citizen.

T aking this exam is a challenge, and so is getting ready for it. Your potential status as a citizen depends on passing the exam, but there are all sorts of pitfalls that can keep you from doing your best. Here are some of the obstacles that can stand in the way of your success:

- being unfamiliar with the format of the exam
- being paralyzed by test anxiety
- leaving your preparation to the last minute or not preparing at all
- not being physically and mentally healthy
- messing up on test day by having to work on an empty stomach or shivering through the exam because the room is cold

What's the common factor in all these test-taking mistakes? One word: control. Who's in control, you or the exam?

Here's the good news: The LearningExpress Test Preparation System puts you in control. In just six easy-to-follow steps, you will learn everything you need to know to make sure that you are in charge of your preparation and your performance on the exam. Other test-takers may let the exam get the better of them; other test-takers may be unprepared—but not you. You will have taken all the steps you need to pass the U.S. Citizenship Exam.

Here's how the LearningExpress Test Preparation System works: The following easy steps lead you through everything you need to know and do to get ready to master your exam. Each of the steps listed below includes both reading about the step and one or more activities. It's important that you do the activities along with the reading, or you won't be getting the full benefit of the system. Each step tells you approximately how much time that step will take you to complete.

Step 1: Get Information	(30 minutes)
Step 2: Conquer Test Anxiety	(20 minutes)
Step 3: Make a Plan	(50 minutes)
Step 4: Reach Your Peak Performance Zone	(10 minutes)
Step 5: Get Your Act Together	(10 minutes)
Step 6: Do It!	(10 minutes)
Total time for complete system:	(130 minutes— 2 hours, 10 minutes)

We estimate that working through the entire system will take you less than two and a half hours, although it's perfectly OK if you work faster or slower. If you can take a whole afternoon or evening to prep, you can work through the whole LearningExpress Test Preparation System in one sitting. Otherwise, you can break it up, and do just one or two steps a day for the next several days. It's up to you—remember, you're in control.

Step 1: Get Information

Time to complete: 30 minutes
Activities: Read "How to Use This Book"

Knowledge is power. The first step in the LearningExpress Test Preparation System is finding out everything you can about the U.S. Citizenship Exam. Reading the first three chapters in this book will provide you with an overview of both the citizenship process and the exam. In addition, the U.S. Citizenship and Immigration Services division of the U.S. Department of Homeland Security has citizenship resources, including a guide to the exam and other material. The more details you can find out about the exam, the more efficiently you will be able to study.

What's on the U.S. Citizenship Exam

The U.S. Citizenship Exam tests you on U.S. government and history, as well as English reading, writing, and comprehension. It is administered in an interview format. The interviewer will ask you 10 questions from the set list of 100 possible civics questions. The interviewer will ask you to read one sentence in English, write one sentence in English, and they will review your N-400 application with you in English. You must answer 60% of the civics questions correctly, and you must be able to correctly read and write the sentences chosen by the interviewer, based on the vocabulary words provided in this book. Finally, you must be able to understand all the questions the interviewer asks you regarding your N-400 application.

Step 2: Conquer Test Anxiety

Time to complete: 20 minutes
Activity: Take the Test Stress Test

Having complete information about the test is the first step in getting control of the exam. Next, you have to overcome one of the biggest obstacles to test success: test anxiety. Test anxiety can not only impair your performance on the exam itself; it can even keep you from preparing properly. In this step, you will learn stress management techniques that will help you succeed on your exam. Learn these strategies now, and practice them as you work through the questions in this book, so they'll be second nature to you by exam day.

Combating Test Anxiety

The first thing you need to know is that a little test anxiety is a good thing. Everyone gets nervous before a big exam—and if that nervousness motivates you to prepare thoroughly, so much the better. In fact, it can even give you a little extra edge—just the kind of edge you need to do well on the exam.

On the following page is the Test Anxiety Quiz. Stop here and answer the questions on that page to find out whether your level of test anxiety is something you should worry about.

Stress Management before the Test

If you feel your level of anxiety getting the best of you in the weeks before the test, here is what you need to do to bring the level down again:

- **Get prepared.** There's nothing like knowing what to expect, and being prepared for it, to put you in control of test anxiety. That's why you're reading this book. Use it faithfully, and remind yourself that you're better prepared than most of the people taking the test.
- **Practice self-confidence.** A positive attitude is a great way to combat test anxiety. This is no time to be humble or shy. Stand in front of the mirror and say to your reflection, "I'm prepared. I'm full of self-confidence. I'm going to pass this exam. I know I can do it." Say it into a tape recorder and play it back once a day. If you hear it often enough, you will believe it.
- **Fight negative messages.** Every time someone starts telling you how hard the exam is, start telling them your self-confidence messages above. If the someone with the negative messages is you—telling yourself that you just can't do this—don't listen. Turn on your tape recorder and listen to your self-confidence messages.
- **Visualize.** Imagine the pride you will have when you become a U.S. citizen. Visualizing success can help make it happen—and it reminds you of why you're doing all this work in preparing for the exam.
- **Exercise.** Physical activity helps calm your body down and focus your mind. Besides, being in good physical shape can actually help you do well on the exam. Go for a run, lift weights, go swimming—and do it regularly.

Stress Management on Test Day

There are several ways you can bring down your level of test stress and anxiety on test day. They'll work best if you practice them in the weeks before the test, so you know which ones work best for you.

- **Deep breathing.** Take a deep breath while you count to five. Hold it for a count of one, and then let it out on a count of five. Repeat several times.
- **Move your body.** Try rolling your head in a circle. Rotate your shoulders. Shake your hands from the wrist. Many people find these movements very relaxing.
- **Visualize again.** Think of the place where you are most relaxed: lying on the beach in the sun, walking through the park, or whatever. Now, close your eyes and imagine you're actually there. If you practice in advance, you will find that you only need a few seconds of this exercise to experience a significant increase in your sense of well-being.

You need to worry about test anxiety only if it is extreme enough to impair your performance. The following questionnaire will provide a diagnosis of your level of test anxiety. In the blank before each statement, write the number that most accurately describes your experience.

0 = Never   1 = Once or twice   2 = Sometimes   3 = Often

_____ I have gotten so nervous before an exam that I simply put down the books and didn't study for it.

_____ I have experienced disabling physical symptoms such as vomiting and severe headaches because I was nervous about an exam.

_____ I have simply not showed up for an exam because I was scared to take it.

_____ I have experienced dizziness and disorientation while taking an exam.

_____ I have had trouble filling in the little circles because my hands were shaking too hard.

_____ I have failed an exam because I was too nervous to complete it.

_____ **Total: Add up the numbers in the blanks above.**

Your Test Anxiety Score

Here are the steps you should take, depending on your score. If you scored:

- **Below 3,** your level of test anxiety is nothing to worry about; it's probably just enough to give you that little extra edge.

- **Between 3 and 6,** your test anxiety may be enough to impair your performance, and you should practice the stress management techniques listed in this chapter to try to bring your test anxiety down to manageable levels.

- **Above 6,** your level of test anxiety is a serious concern. In addition to practicing the stress management techniques listed in this chapter, you may want to seek additional, personal help. Call your local high school or community college and ask for the academic counselor. Tell the counselor that you have a level of test anxiety that sometimes keeps you from being able to take the exam. The counselor may be willing to help you or may suggest someone else you should talk to.

When anxiety threatens to overwhelm you *during the exam*, there are still things you can do to manage the stress level:

- **Repeat your self-confidence messages.** You should have them memorized by now. Say them quietly to yourself, and believe them!
- **Visualize one more time.** This time, visualize yourself answering the exam questions confidently and correctly. Like most visualization techniques, this one works best if you've practiced it ahead of time.

Try these techniques ahead of time, and see if they work for you!

Step 3: Make a Plan

Time to complete: 50 minutes
Activity: Construct a study plan

Maybe the most important thing you can do to get control of yourself and your exam is to make a study plan. Too many people fail to prepare simply because they fail to plan. Spending hours on the day before the exam poring over the 100 questions not only raises your level of test anxiety, it is simply no substitute for careful preparation and practice over time.

Don't fall into the cram trap. Take control of your preparation time by mapping out a study schedule. Depending on the amount of time you have before the exam, determine how much time you will devote to studying each week or, preferably, each day. If you're the kind of person who needs deadlines and assignments to motivate you for a project, lay them out in calendar form.

Even more important than making a plan is making a commitment. You can't learn U.S. civics and history overnight. You have to set aside some time every day for study and practice. Try for at least 20 minutes a day. Twenty minutes daily will do you much more good than two hours crammed into a Saturday.

If you have months before the exam, you're lucky. Don't put off your study until the week before the exam! Start now. Even ten minutes a day, with half an hour or more on weekends, can make a big difference in your performance.

Step 4: Reach Your Peak Performance Zone

Time to complete: 10 minutes to read; weeks to complete!
Activity: Complete the Physical Preparation Checklist

To get ready for a challenge like the U.S. Citizenship Exam, you have to take control of your physical, as well as your mental, state. Exercise, proper diet, and rest will ensure that your body works with, rather than against, your mind on test day, as well as during your preparation.

Exercise

If you don't already have a regular exercise program going, the time during which you're preparing for an exam is actually an excellent time to start one. And if you're already keeping fit—or trying to get that way—don't let the pressure of preparing for an exam fool you into quitting now. Exercise helps reduce stress by pumping wonderful good-feeling hormones called endorphins into your system. It also increases the oxygen supply throughout your body, including your brain, so you will be at peak performance on test day.

A half hour of vigorous activity—enough to raise a sweat—every day should be your aim. If you're really pressed for time, every other day is OK. Choose an activity you like and get out there and do it. Jogging with a friend always makes the time go faster, or take a radio.

But don't overdo it. You don't want to exhaust yourself. Moderation is the key.

Diet

First of all, cut out the junk. Go easy on caffeine and nicotine, and eliminate alcohol and any other drugs from your system at least two weeks before the exam.

What your body needs for peak performance is simply a balanced diet. Eat plenty of fruits and vegetables, along with protein and carbohydrates. Foods that are high in lecithin (an amino acid), such as fish and beans, are especially good brain foods.

The night before the exam, you might carbo-load the way athletes do before a contest. Eat a big plate of spaghetti, rice and beans, or whatever your favorite carbohydrate is.

Rest

You probably know how much sleep you need every night to be at your best, even if you don't always get it. Make sure you do get that much sleep, though, for at least a week before the exam. Moderation is important here, too. Too much sleep will just make you groggy.

If you're not a morning person and your exam appointment is in the morning, you should reset your internal clock so that your body doesn't think you're taking an exam at 3 A.M. You have to start this process well before the exam. The way it works is to get up half an hour earlier each morning, and then go to bed half an hour earlier that night. Don't try it the other way around; you will just toss and turn if you go to bed early without having gotten up early. The next morning, get up another half an hour earlier, and so on. How long you will have to do this depends on how late you're used to getting up. Use the Physical Preparation Checklist on the following page to make sure you're in tip-top form.

Step 5: Get Your Act Together

Time to complete: 10 minutes to read; time to complete will vary

Activity: Complete Final Preparations worksheet

You're in control of your mind and body; you're in charge of test anxiety, your preparation, and your test-taking strategies. Now, it's time to take charge of external factors, like the testing site and the materials you need to take the exam.

Find Out Where the Exam Is and Make a Trial Run

The USCIS will notify you when and where your exam is being held. Do you know how to get to the location? Do you know how long it will take to get there? If not, make a trial run, preferably on the same day of the week at the same time of day. Make note on the Final Preparations worksheet on page 27, of the amount of time it will take you to get to the exam site. Plan on arriving 10–15 minutes early so you can get the lay of the land, use the bathroom, and calm down. Then figure out how early you will have to get up that morning, and make sure you get up that early every day for a week before the exam.

Gather Your Materials

The night before the exam, lay out the clothes you will wear and the materials you have to bring with you to the exam. Plan on dressing in layers; you won't have any control over the temperature of the examination room. Have a sweater or jacket you can take off if it's warm. Use the checklist on the Final Preparations worksheet to help you pull together what you will need.

PHYSICAL PREPARATION CHECKLIST

For the week before the test, write down what physical exercise you engaged in and for how long, and what you ate for each meal. Remember, you're trying for at least half an hour of exercise every other day (preferably every day) and a balanced diet that's light on junk food.

Exam minus 7 days

Exercise: _____ for _____ minutes

Breakfast: _____

Lunch: _____

Dinner: _____

Snacks: _____

Exam minus 6 days

Exercise: _____ for _____ minutes

Breakfast: _____

Lunch: _____

Dinner: _____

Snacks: _____

Exam minus 5 days

Exercise: _____ for _____ minutes

Breakfast: _____

Lunch: _____

Dinner: _____

Snacks: _____

Exam minus 4 days

Exercise: _____ for _____ minutes

Breakfast: _____

Lunch: _____

Dinner: _____

Snacks: _____

Exam minus 3 days

Exercise: _____ for _____ minutes

Breakfast: _____

Lunch: _____

Dinner: _____

Snacks: _____

Exam minus 2 days

Exercise: _____ for _____ minutes

Breakfast: _____

Lunch: _____

Dinner: _____

Snacks: _____

Exam minus 1 day

Exercise: _____ for _____ minutes

Breakfast: _____

Lunch: _____

Dinner: _____

Snacks: _____

Don't Skip Breakfast

Even if you don't usually eat breakfast, do so on exam morning. A cup of coffee doesn't count. Don't do doughnuts or other sweet foods, either. A sugar high will leave you with a sugar low in the middle of the exam. A mix of protein and carbohydrates is best: cereal with milk and just a little sugar, or eggs with toast, will do your body a world of good.

Step 6: Do It!

Time to complete: 10 minutes, plus test-taking time
Activity: Pass the U.S. Citizenship Exam!

Fast forward to exam day. You're ready. You made a study plan and followed through. You practiced your test-taking strategies while working through this book. You're in control of your physical, mental, and emotional state. You know when and where to show up and what to bring with you. In other words, you're prepared for the exam.

Now you can go into the exam, full of confidence, armed with test-taking strategies you've practiced until they're second nature. You're in control of yourself, your environment, and your performance on the exam. You're ready to succeed. So do it. Go in there and pass the exam. And look forward to your future as a U.S. citizen!

Getting to the Exam Site

Location of exam site: _____

Date: _____

Departure time: _____

Do I know how to get to the exam site?   Yes ____   No ____

(If no, make a trial run.)

Time it will take to get to exam site: _____

Things to Lay Out the Night Before

Clothes I will wear   ____

Sweater/jacket   ____

Watch   ____

Photo ID   ____

Other Things to Bring/Remember

_____

_____

_____

_____

_____

_____

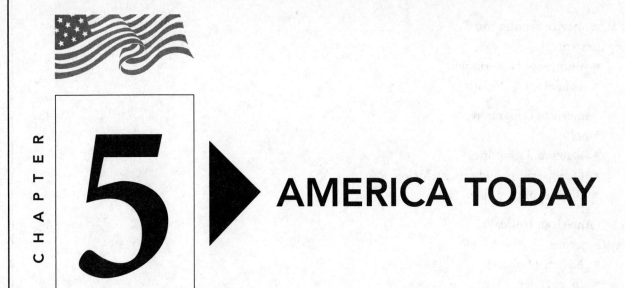

5 ▶ AMERICA TODAY

I n this chapter, we look at some of the important people and aspects of government in America today. We also review the symbols of America—the U.S. flag and the national anthem. We start by covering a few questions about citizenship and voting.

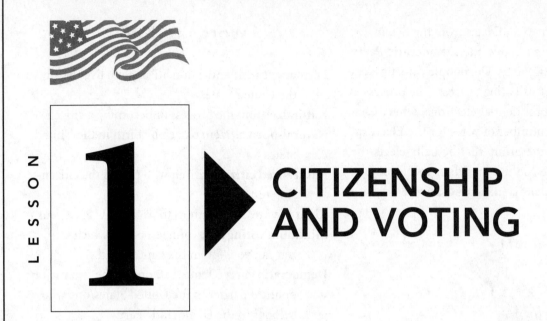

1 ▶ CITIZENSHIP AND VOTING

There are different paths to citizenship in the United States. Most Americans have been citizens for their entire lives, because they were born in America. People who love America but were not born here can also become citizens through the process of **naturalization**. Immigrants to the United States may apply to become American citizens after living in the United States as a **permanent resident** for five years. Immigrants that are married to U.S. citizens may apply for citizenship after being a permanent resident for three years.

Both **natural-born citizens and naturalized citizens** have all the rights and benefits that come with citizenship. The benefits to becoming a U.S. citizen include the right to vote, the right to travel with a U.S. passport, the right to serve on a jury, and the right to apply for federal jobs and to petition for close relatives to come to the United States to live. Voting and serving on a jury are important responsibilities of American citizens, and they are two rights that only citizens have. In addition to voting and serving on juries, American citizens have other important responsibilities, such as paying federal income taxes by **April 15** and registering for the **Selective Service**, which all males over 18 must do.

However, the most important right granted to U.S. citizens is the **right to vote**. This right is guaranteed to all citizens over the age of 18 by the Constitution, in amendments 14, 15, 19, 24, and 26. Starting from the **minimum voting age** of 18, American citizens can help choose which candidates will take office in government. The elections usually have candidates from the two major parties in the United States: the **Democratic Party** and the **Republican Party**. **The people** directly elect Congress through this voting process. The process is more indirect in presidential elections, where each state has a certain number of votes for the **Electoral College**, which is the group that actually elects the president. We vote for the president in November, and the new president is inaugurated, or sworn into office, in January.

Vote in November

President inaugurated in January

Words to Know

Permanent resident: a noncitizen who lives legally in the United States

Naturalization: the process of becoming a citizen

Natural-born citizen: citizen by birth in the United States

Naturalized citizen: citizen who passed the citizenship test

Right to vote: most important right of U.S. citizens

Minimum voting age: youngest age at which a citizen can vote (18 in the United States)

Democratic Party/Democrat: one of the two major political parties in the United States/one who belongs to the Democratic Party

Republican Party/Republican: one of the two major political parties in the United States/one who belongs to the Republican Party

Electoral College: group that actually elects the president

The people: directly elect members of Congress

Related Questions

1. **Q:** Name one benefit of being a citizen.
A: One benefit is the ability . . . (choose one from below)

- **to obtain federal government jobs**
- **to travel with a U.S. passport**
- **to petition for close relatives to come to the United States to live**
- **to serve on a jury**
- **to vote**

2. **Q:** Name one important responsibility that is reserved especially for citizens.
A: Citizens can **vote** and **serve on a jury**.

3. **Q:** What is the minimum voting age in the United States?
A: The minimum voting age in the United States is **18**.

4. **Q:** What are you promising to do when you become a citizen?
A: You are promising to **give up loyalty to other countries**, **defend the Constitution** and **laws of the United States**, and **be loyal to the United States**.

5. **Q:** Who elects Congress?
A: **The people** elect Congress directly.

6. **Q:** Who elects the president of the United States?
A: **The Electoral College** elects the president of the United States.

7. **Q:** What are the two major political parties in the United States?
A: The two major political parties are **the Democratic** and **Republican parties**.

8. **Q:** When are your federal income taxes due?
A: Federal income taxes are due on **April 15**.

9. **Q:** When must all men register for the Selective Service?
A: All men must register for the Selective Service at **age 18**.

10. **Q:** Describe one amendment to the Constitution that deals with who can vote.
A: Citizens 18 and older can vote. You don't have to pay to vote. **Any citizen can vote.**

11. **Q:** What are two ways that Americans can participate in their democracy?
A: Vote, join a political party, help with a campaign, join a civic group/community group, give an elected official your opinion on an issue or policy, run for office, write to a newspaper.

Exercises

Fill in the Blank

The answers to these five questions can be found on page 96.

1. The president of the United States is elected in _____.

2. You must be at least _____ years old to vote in the United States.

3. The two major political parties in America are the _____ and the _____ parties.

4. The right to _____ is the most important right granted to American citizens.

5. Congress is directly _____ by the people.

Multiple Choice

Choose the best answer for each question. Answers can be found on page 96.

1. Men must register for the Selective Service at age
   a. 21
   b. 30
   c. 18
   d. 16

2. A noncitizen who lives legally in the United States is called a
   a. permanent resident
   b. visiting resident
   c. sub-citizen
   d. permanent visitor

3. Which of the following is **not** a benefit solely of being a citizen?
   a. being able to vote
   b. being able to serve on a jury
   c. being able to obtain a drivers license
   d. being able to travel with the U.S. passport

Reading and Writing Exercises

The following vocabulary words will be tested on the exam. The words will be spoken out loud to you by the interviewer, and you will need to write them down on a piece of paper. Practice **writing** each sentence below, making sure you know how to spell each word correctly.

WRITING VOCABULARY

right	November
citizen	to
elect	can
people	for
pay	the
taxes	want
vote	we
President	in

Citizens can vote.

_____

We pay taxes.

_____

Citizens pay taxes.

_____

People want to vote.

_____

We vote for the President in November.

_____

Citizens can vote for the President in November.

_____

The following vocabulary words will be tested on the exam. The words will be written down on a piece of paper, and you will be asked to read them out loud to the interviewer during the exam. Practice **reading** each sentence opposite out loud, making sure you can pronounce all words correctly.

READING VOCABULARY

right	when
citizen	what
elects	do
vote	we
people	for
President	can
pay	to
who	want

Who can vote?

When do we vote for President?

What do we pay?

Citizens elect the President.

People elect the President.

People want the right to vote.

LESSON 2 ▶ SYMBOLS OF AMERICA

Perhaps the most visible symbol of America is the **red**, **white**, and **blue American flag**. The **13 red** and **white stripes** represent the original 13 states, which were called **colonies**. The **50 white stars** signify the 50 states in the union now. However, besides representing America's past and present, the flag is also a symbol of freedom and the American spirit.

For example, our **national anthem**, called **"The Star-Spangled Banner,"** salutes the flag. It was written during the War of 1812. The anthem describes how the waving flag provided hope during an important battle, because it represents America—"the land of the free and the home of the brave."

The **Pledge of Allegiance** also declares loyalty to the American flag and the country it represents. Another important symbol of America is the **Statue of Liberty**. The Statue of Liberty was a gift from France in 1886. The statue is of a woman holding a torch in one hand and a book in the other, and it stands on Liberty Island, near New York's Ellis Island in New York Harbor. It has welcomed the many immigrants who entered the United States at Ellis Island, as the first visible symbol of the hope and freedom that America promises.

The Statue of Liberty

The American flag

The Pledge of Allegiance

I pledge allegiance, to the flag
of the United States of America.
And to the republic, for which it stands
One nation, under God, indivisible
With liberty and justice for all.

The Star-Spangled Banner

O say, can you see, by the Dawn's early light?
What so proudly we hailed at the twilight's last
* gleaming?*
Whose broad stripes and bright stars, through the per-
* ilous fight,*
O'er the ramparts we watched, were so gallantly
* streaming?*
And the rockets' red glare, the bombs bursting in air,
Gave proof through the night that our flag was still
* there*
O say, does that star-spangled banner yet wave
O'er the land of the free and the home of the brave?

Words to Know

American flag: a symbol of America that is red,
white, and blue

Red, white, and blue: the colors of the flag

Stars: 50 stars on the American flag, representing the
number of states in the Union

Stripes: 13 stripes on the American flag, representing
the original states

National anthem: the country's official song

"The Star-Spangled Banner": American national
anthem

Colonies: original 13 states in America

Related Questions

1. Q: What are the colors of the American flag?
A: The colors of the American flag are **red**, **white**, and **blue**.

2. Q: Why are there 50 stars on the flag?
A: There are 50 stars on the flag because **there are 50 states**, and each star represents one state.

3. Q: Why are there 13 stripes on the flag?
A: There are 13 stripes on the flag because **there were 13 original colonies**, and each stripe represents one original colony.

4. Q: Who do we show loyalty to when we say the Pledge of Allegiance?
A: We show loyalty to **the United States**, or **the flag of the United States**.

5. Q: Where is the Statue of Liberty located?
A: The Statue of Liberty is located on Liberty Island, near **Ellis Island**.

6. Q: What is the national anthem of the United States?
A: The national anthem of the United States is **"The Star-Spangled Banner."**

7. Q: How many states are there in the union?
A: There are **50** states in the union.

8. Q: Name the 13 original colonies.
A: The colonies were Connecticut, Delaware, Georgia, Maryland, Massachusetts, New Hampshire, New Jersey, New York, North Carolina, Pennsylvania, Rhode Island, South Carolina, and Virginia.

Exercises

Fill in the Blank

The answers to these four questions can be found on page 96.

1. The colors of the flag are _____, _____, and _____.

2. The stars on the flag represent _____.

3. The _____ on the flag represent the 13 original colonies.

4. Our national anthem is called _____.

Multiple Choice

Choose the best answer for each question. Answers can be found on page 96.

1. The United States has how many states?
   a. 13
   b. 50
   c. 26
   d. 48

2. Which of the following was **not** one of the original 13 colonies?
   a. New Hampshire
   b. New York
   c. Virginia
   d. Main

3. "The Star-Spangled Banner" is the
   a. American hymn
   b. National anthem
   c. Pledge of allegiance
   d. Anthem of peace

Reading and Writing Exercises

The following vocabulary words will be tested on the exam. The words will be spoken out loud to you by the interviewer, and you will need to write them down on a piece of paper. Practice **writing** each sentence below, making sure you know how to spell each word correctly.

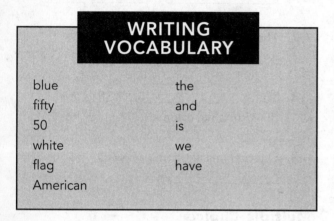

WRITING VOCABULARY

blue	the
fifty	and
50	is
white	we
flag	have
American	

The flag is red, white, and blue.

_____

The American flag is red, white, and blue.

_____

We have 50/fifty states

_____

The following vocabulary words will be tested on the exam. The words will be written down on a piece of paper, and you will be asked to read them out loud to the interviewer during the exam. Practice **reading** each sentence below out loud, making sure you can pronounce all words correctly.

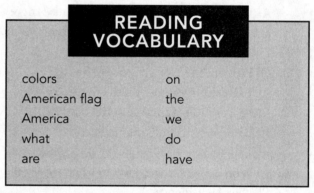

READING VOCABULARY

colors	on
American flag	the
America	we
what	do
are	have

What colors are on the American Flag?

How many states do we have?

LESSON 3 ▶ AMERICA AROUND YOU

Abraham Lincoln called the American system of government a "government of the people, by the people, and for the people." While the people do not all directly make decisions in government, American citizens do choose their leaders by voting for candidates, who usually come from the two major political parties: the **Democrats** and the **Republicans**. This system of representative government is called a **democratic republic**. The government is based in the capital of the United States, **Washington, D.C.**

In the American system of government, power is divided up by checks and balances between the three **branches** of government: **legislative**, **executive**, and **judicial**. The legislative branch makes laws, the executive branch enforces the laws, and the judicial branch interprets the laws through the court system. At the federal level, the legislative branch is Congress, the executive branch is the president and the cabinet, and the judicial branch is the Supreme Court. The system of **checks and balances** prevents any one branch of government from becoming too powerful. You will learn more about the three branches of government in Chapter 6.

You may have heard of **President Donald Trump**, **Vice President Mike Pence**, and **Supreme Court Chief Justice John Roberts**. (Note: These names and titles were accurate at the time this book was published.) However, your state and local officials serve important roles as well. A governor is in charge of running the government of a state. Who is your governor? Do you know your state's senators?

In addition to the system of government, the economic system is an important aspect of the country that you live in. The United States has a **capitalist economy** that is based on **free markets**.

Three branches of government

Words to Know

Democratic republic: system of government in which citizens elect representatives to govern

Washington, D.C.: the capital of the United States

Branch: part

Legislative: branch of government that makes federal laws

Executive: branch of government that enforces laws

Judicial: branch of government that interprets the laws

President: chief executive of the federal government

Governor: head executive of a state

Checks and balances: system that prevents one branch of the government from becoming too powerful

Capitalist economy: economic system that the United States uses; based on free markets

Related Questions

1. **Q:** What kind of government does the United States have?
A: The U.S. government is a **democratic republic**.

2. **Q:** How many branches are there in our government?
A: There are **three** branches.

3. **Q:** What are the three branches of our government?
A: The three branches of government are the **legislative**, **executive**, and **judicial**.

4. **Q:** Who are the two senators from your state?
A: My senators are _____ and _____. (Look up your state's senators.)

5. **Q:** What is the capital of your state?
A: My state's capital is _____. (Look up your state's capital.)

6. **Q:** Who is the governor of your state?
A: My governor is _____. (Look up your state's governor.)

7. **Q:** What stops one branch of government from becoming too powerful?
A: The system of checks and balances prevents one branch of government from becoming too powerful.

8. **Q:** Who is your U.S. representative?
A: My U.S. representative is _____. (Look up your U.S. representative.)

9. **Q:** What kind of economic system do we have in the United States?
A: We have a **capitalist economy** in the United States.

10. Q: How many states are there in the union?
A: There are _____ states in the union.

11. Q: What are the two major political parties in the United States?
A: The two major political parties in the United States are the _____ and the _____.

Exercises

Fill in the Blank

The answers to these five questions can be found on page 96.

1. _____ keeps any one branch of government from becoming too powerful.

2. The _____ branch of government makes the federal laws.

3. _____ is the capital of the United States of America.

4. The system of government of the United States in which citizens elect representatives to govern them is a _____.

5. The _____, the vice president, and the _____ make up the executive branch.

Multiple Choice

Choose the best answer for each question. Answers can be found on page 96.

1. Which of the following is **not** one of the three branches of government?
   a. legislative
   b. executive
   c. economic
   d. judicial

2. A governor is the
   a. head executive of a city.
   b. leader of congress.
   c. head executive of state.
   d. head executive of a county.

3. How many senators does each state have?
   a. A number that varies depending on population
   b. 1
   c. 5
   d. 2

Reading and Writing Exercises

The following vocabulary words will be tested on the exam. The words will be spoken out loud to you by the interviewer, and you will need to write them down on a piece of paper. Practice **writing** each sentence below, making sure you know how to spell each word correctly.

WRITING VOCABULARY

capital	the
President	in
Washington D.C.	is
lives	Congress
Washington	meets

The President lives in Washington D.C.

_____

The President lives in the White House.

_____

The White House is in Washington D.C.

_____

Congress meets in Washington.

_____

The following vocabulary words will be tested on the exam. The words will be written down on a piece of paper, and you will be asked to read them out loud to the interviewer during the exam. Practice **reading** each sentence opposite out loud, making sure you can pronounce all words correctly.

READING VOCABULARY

President	the
White House	is
live	who
where	Washington D.C.
in	does

Who lives in Washington D.C.?

Who lives in the White House?

Where is the White House?

Where does the President live?

4 ▶ AMERICAN GEOGRAPHY

The United States is a large country with an interesting geography. With a land mass of 9.8 million square kilometers, the United States is the second largest country in North America. Canada is the largest country with a land mass of 9.9 million square kilometers. The United States borders **Canada** to the north and **Mexico** to the south. Some of the states that border Canada are **Maine**, **New York**, **Minnesota**, **North Dakota**, **Montana**, and **Washington**. The states that have borders with Mexico are **Texas**, **New Mexico**, **Arizona**, and **California**. The country has large oceans on either side of it. The **Atlantic Ocean** lies on the east coast of the United States, and the **Pacific Ocean** lies on the west coast.

The country is made up of 50 states, **Washington, D.C.**, and five territories. The capital of the United States is Washington, D.C. Every state has a capital as well. Do you know the capital of your state? The U.S. territories are **Puerto Rico**, **Guam**, **the U.S. Virgin Islands**, **the Northern Mariana Islands**, and **American Samoa**.

Because the United States is so big, its land has many interesting features, including rivers and mountains. The longest rivers in the country are the **Mississippi** and the **Missouri**, which run through the center of the country. The highest mountain is **Mt. McKinley**, or **Denali**, which is located in Alaska.

Words to Know

Atlantic Ocean: ocean on the east coast of the United States

Pacific Ocean: ocean on the west coast of the United States

Mississippi River: longest river in the United States

Washington, D.C.: capital of the United States

Canada: the country to the north of the United States

Mexico: the country to the south of the United States

Related Questions

1. **Q:** On what continent is the United States located?
   A: The United States is located on **North America**.

2. **Q:** What ocean is on the east coast of the United States?
   A: The **Atlantic Ocean** is on the east coast of the United States.

3. **Q:** What ocean is on the west coast of the United States?
   A: The **Pacific Ocean** is on the west coast of the United States.

4. **Q:** Name one U.S. territory.
   A: U.S. territories include **Puerto Rico, Guam, U.S. Virgin Islands, Northern Mariana Islands**, and **American Samoa**.

5. **Q:** What is the tallest mountain in the United States?
   A: The tallest mountain in the United States is **Mt. McKinley (Denali)**.

6. **Q:** What are the longest rivers in the United States?
   A: The longest rivers in the United States are the **Mississippi River** and the **Missouri River**.

7. **Q:** Name one state that borders Canada.
   A: The states that border Canada include **Maine, New York, Minnesota, North Dakota, Montana**, and **Washington**.

8. **Q:** Name one state that borders Mexico.
   A: The states that border Mexico include **California, New Mexico, Arizona**, and **Texas**.

9. **Q:** What is the capital of the United States?
   A: The capital of the United States is **Washington, D.C.**

Exercises

Fill in the Blank

The answers to these five questions can be found on page 96.

1. The United States is bordered by _____ to the north and _____ to the south.

2. Guam and Puerto Rico are examples of United States _____.

3. The Mississippi and the Missouri are the country's two longest _____.

4. Minnesota is a state that borders _____.

5. California is a state that borders _____.

Multiple Choice

Choose the best answer for each question. Answers can be found on page 96.

1. How many territories does the United States have?
   a. 50
   b. 5
   c. none
   d. 13

2. What is the capital of the United States?
   a. Texas
   b. New York
   c. Washington, D.C.
   d. Liberty Island

3. Guam is
   a. the 50th U.S. state.
   b. A U.S. territory.
   c. the country that borders California to the south.
   d. the capital of Florida.

Reading and Writing Exercises

The following vocabulary words will be tested on the exam. The words will be spoken out loud to you by the interviewer, and you will need to write them down on a piece of paper. Practice **writing** each sentence, making sure you know how to spell each word correctly.

WRITING VOCABULARY

Alaska	50
largest	states
California	is
Canada	the
Delaware	first
Mexico	capital
New York City	was
United States	of
north	has
south	we
fifty	

Alaska is the largest state in the United States.

_____

Alaska is the largest U.S. state.

_____

New York City was the first capital of the United States.

_____

Canada is north of the United States.

_____

Mexico is south of the United States.

_____

California has the most people.

_____

We have 50/fifty states.

_____

Delaware was the first state.

_____

The following vocabulary words will be tested on the exam. The words will be written down on a piece of paper, and you will be asked to read them out loud to the interviewer during the exam. Practice **reading** each sentence opposite out loud, making sure you can pronounce all words correctly.

READING VOCABULARY

capital	has
country	have
north	the
south	is
state	of
people	first
White House	how
United States	many
U.S.	do
what	we

What state has the most people?

What country is north of the United States?

What country is south of the United States?

What city was the first capital of the U.S.?

How many states do we have?

What was the first state?

LESSON

5 ▶ AMERICAN HOLIDAYS

American people celebrate several important national **holidays** that occur throughout the year. Perhaps the most important holiday is **Independence Day**, which we celebrate on July 4 to celebrate the country's independence from Great Britain. Other important holidays are **Veterans Day** and **Memorial Day**, which celebrate people who have fought for the country in wars; **Thanksgiving**, a celebration of the pilgrims' friendship with the Native Americans; **Presidents Day**, also celebrated as Washington's birthday; and **Martin Luther King, Jr., Day**, which honors an important American who you will read about soon.

Words to Know

Holiday: a special day of celebration for everyone in the country
Independence Day: the celebration of America's independence from Great Britain, celebrated on July 4

Related Questions

1. **Q:** When do we celebrate Independence Day?
   A: We celebrate Independence Day on **July 4**.

2. **Q:** Can you name the other national holidays that America celebrates?
   A: Thanksgiving, Memorial Day, Veterans Day, Martin Luther King, Jr. Day, New Year's Day, Presidents Day, Labor Day, Columbus Day, and Christmas.

Exercises

Fill in the Blank

The answers to these questions can be found on page 96.

1. The important holiday on July 4 is
   _____.

2. Thanksgiving, Veterans Day, and Memorial Day are all examples of _____.

Reading and Writing Exercises

The following vocabulary words will be tested on the exam. The words will be spoken out loud to you by the interviewer, and you will need to write them down on a piece of paper. Practice **writing** each sentence, making sure you know how to spell each word correctly.

WRITING VOCABULARY

February	Memorial Day
May	Flag Day
June	Independence Day
July	Labor Day
September	Columbus Day
October	Thanksgiving
November	is
Presidents Day	in

Columbus Day is in October.

_____

Independence Day is in July.

_____

Thanksgiving is in November.

_____

Labor Day is in September.

_____

Flag Day is in June.

_____

Memorial Day is in May.

_____

President's Day is in February.

_____

The following vocabulary words will be tested on the exam. The words will be written down on a piece of paper, and you will be asked to read them out loud to the interviewer during the exam. Practice **reading** each sentence opposite out loud, making sure you can pronounce all words correctly.

READING VOCABULARY

Presidents Day   Columbus Day
Memorial Day   Thanksgiving
Flag Day   when
Independence Day   is
Labor Day

When is President's Day?

When is Memorial Day?

When is Independence Day?

When is Labor Day?

When is Columbus Day?

When is Thanksgiving?

6 ▶ AMERICAN HISTORY

This chapter will teach you some basics about United States history. It starts with the birth of the United States and covers the major wars and movements, from the American Revolution to the civil rights movement.

Lesson 8:   The Civil War and Modern History   65

Key Concepts:

- The Civil War
- Abraham Lincoln and the Emancipation Proclamation
- World War I and World War II
- Alaska and Hawaii
- Dr. Martin Luther King, Jr., and the civil rights movement

6 ▶ THE 13 COLONIES

The history of the United States government begins with the **13 original states**, which were called **colonies.** These states were settled by groups of colonists who came to America from Great Britain. The **pilgrims** were the first of these American colonists, and they came to America for **religious freedom**. When they arrived in America, the winters were very hard. It was only with the help of the **Native Americans (or American Indians)** that the pilgrims survived. To give thanks for their help and for their new homes, the colonists celebrated **Thanksgiving** with the Native Americans. Some of the Native American tribes are named the **Cherokee, Navajo, Sioux, Apache**, and **Creek**, but there are many more as well.

In all, there were **13 colonies: Connecticut, Delaware, Georgia, Maryland, Massachusetts, New Hampshire, New Jersey, New York, North Carolina, Pennsylvania, Rhode Island, South Carolina**, and **Virginia**. The king of Great Britain, King George III, ruled the colonies.

The 13 colonies

Words to Know

Colonies: the 13 original states

Pilgrims: the first American colonists

Religious freedom: being allowed to practice any religion

Native Americans (American Indians): people who lived in America before the pilgrims arrived

Thanksgiving: holiday celebrated for the first time by the American colonists to thank the Native Americans

The colonies sought freedom from England

Related Questions

1. **Q:** Why did the pilgrims come to America?
   A: The pilgrims came to America for **religious freedom**.

2. **Q:** Who lived in America before the pilgrims arrived?
   A: **The Native Americans**, or **American Indians**, lived in America before the pilgrims arrived.

3. **Q:** Name a Native American tribe.
   A: The Native American tribes include the **Cherokee, Navajo, Sioux, Apache, Creek, Chippewa, Choctaw, Pueblo, Iroquois, Blackfeet, Seminole, Cheyenne, Arawak, Shawnee, Mohegan, Huron, Oneida, Lakota, Crow, Teton, Hopi, Inuit.**

4. **Q:** What holiday was celebrated for the first time by the American colonists?
   A: **Thanksgiving** was celebrated for the first time by the American colonists.

5. **Q:** What were the 13 original states called?
   A: The 13 original states were called **the 13 colonies**.

6. Q: Can you name the 13 original states?

A: The 13 original states were **Connecticut, Delaware, Georgia, Maryland, Massachusetts, New Hampshire, New Jersey, New York, North Carolina, Pennsylvania, Rhode Island, South Carolina,** and **Virginia**

Pilgrims

Exercises

Fill in the Blank

The answers to these five questions can be found on page 97.

1. The _____ were the first American colonists.

2. The 13 original states were called _____.

3. The _____ lived in America before the colonists arrived.

4. _____ is the holiday that was first celebrated by the American colonists.

5. The pilgrims came to America for _____.

Reading and Writing Exercises

The following vocabulary words will be tested on the exam. The words will be spoken out loud to you by the interviewer, and you will need to write them down on a piece of paper. Practice **writing** each sentence below, making sure you know how to spell each word correctly.

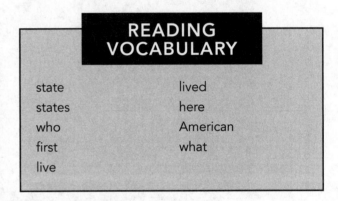

WRITING VOCABULARY	
American Indians	America
lived	was
first	the
here	in
Delaware	state

American Indians lived here first.

_____

Delaware was the first state.

_____

American Indians lived in America.

_____

The following vocabulary words will be tested on the exam. The words will be written down on a piece of paper, and you will be asked to read them out loud to the interviewer during the exam. Practice **reading** each sentence below out loud, making sure you can pronounce all words correctly.

READING VOCABULARY	
state	lived
states	here
who	American
first	what
live	

Who lived here first?

What was the first state?

LESSON

7 ▶ THE AMERICAN REVOLUTION

The colonies did not like being ruled by King George III, because they had no say in government but still had to pay taxes to Great Britain. So the American colonists decided to fight for their freedom from Great Britain.

On July 4, 1776, the American colonies adopted the **Declaration of Independence**, which **Thomas Jefferson** and others had written. The basic beliefs of the Declaration are that **all men are created equal** and that all people have the right to life, liberty, and the pursuit of happiness. This started the **Revolutionary War**, also known as the **American Revolution**. In the United States, **Independence Day** is a federal holiday celebrated every **July 4**, signifying the United States' declaration of independence from the kingdom of Great Britain.

George Washington was the first **commander in chief** of the new country's army. Under Washington's leadership, the U.S. army defeated the English in 1783. George Washington was unanimously elected the first president of the United States. For his important role in American history, George Washington is known as the **"father of our country."**

After the United States achieved independence, its leaders met in 1787 to write a **Constitution** (this is discussed more in Lesson 9). This was called the **Constitutional Convention**. One important member of this convention was **Benjamin Franklin**. He was the oldest member of the convention, a U.S. diplomat, the first postmaster general of the United States, and the author of *Poor Richard's Almanac*. Before the Constitution was ratified, the **Federalist Papers** explained the purpose and meaning of the proposed Constitution, and promoted ratification. They were written by **James Madison**, **Alexander Hamilton**, and **John Jay**, but were published under the pseudonym, or fictitious name, **"Publius."**

Thomas Jefferson

Words to Know

Declaration of Independence: document written in 1776 declaring independence from Great Britain

Thomas Jefferson: main writer of the Declaration of Independence

All men are created equal: basic belief of the Declaration of Independence

Revolutionary War, or American Revolution: war to fight for freedom from Great Britain

Independence Day: a federal holiday celebrated July 4; celebrates the declaration of independence from Great Britain

George Washington: first commander in chief and president, father of our country

Benjamin Franklin: oldest delegate at the Constitutional Convention; he was also a diplomat, the postmaster general, and the author of *Poor Richard's Almanac*

Federalist Papers: documents that supported the passage of the Constitution, written by Alexander Hamilton, James Madison, and John Jay (Publius)

Signing the Declaration of Independence

Relevant Questions

1. Q: What country did America fight during the Revolutionary War?
A: America fought **Great Britain** during the Revolutionary War.

2. Q: What did the Declaration of Independence do?
A: The **Declaration of Independence announced our independence from Great Britain.**

3. Q: What is the date of Independence Day?
A: Independence Day is on **July 4.**

4. Q: Independence Day celebrates independence from whom?
A: Independence Day celebrates independence from **Great Britain.**

5. Q: When was the Declaration of Independence adopted?
A: The Declaration of Independence was adopted on **July 4, 1776.**

6. Q: What are the three rights in the Declaration of Independence?
A: The three rights include **life**, **liberty**, and the **pursuit of happiness.**

7. Q: Who was the main writer of the Declaration of Independence?
A: **Thomas Jefferson** was the main writer of the Declaration of Independence.

8. Q: Who was the first president of the United States?
A: **George Washington** was the first president of the United States.

9. Q: Which president is called the "father of our country"?
A: **George Washington** is called the "father of our country."

10. Q: Which president was the first commander in chief of the U.S. Army?
A: **George Washington** was the first commander in chief of the U.S. Army.

11. Q: What makes Benjamin Franklin famous?
A: Benjamin Franklin was **the oldest member of the Constitutional Convention, the first postmaster general of the United States, a U.S. diplomat,** and **the author of** *Poor Richard's Almanac.*

12. Q: Name one of the writers of the Federalist Papers.
A: The writers of the Federalist Papers included **Alexander Hamilton**, **James Madison**, and **John Jay (Publius).**

13. Q: What is one reason that colonists came to America?
A: Freedom, political liberty, religious freedom, economic opportunity, to escape persecution, to practice their religion.

14. Q: Why did the colonists fight the British?
A: They fought the British because of high taxes, the British army stayed in their houses, and they didn't have self-government.

Exercises

Fill in the Blank

The answers to these six questions can be found on page 97.

1. The Declaration of Independence was adopted on _____.

2. Alexander Hamilton and John Jay were two of the writers of _____.

3. The oldest member of the Constitutional Convention was _____.

4. The main writer of the Declaration of Independence was _____.

5. _____ was the first commander in chief of the U.S. Army.

6. One of the main beliefs of the _____ is that all men are created equal.

Multiple Choice

Choose the best answer for each question. Answers can be found on page 97.

1. Which of the following statements about George Washington is **not** true?
   a. He is called the "father of our country."
   b. He was the first commander in chief of the U.S. Army
   c. He wrote the Federalist Papers.
   d. He was the first president of the United States.

2. What was the war to fight for freedom from Great Britain called?
   a. The Civil War
   b. The American Revolution
   c. The British War
   d. The Great War

3. When was the Constitutional Convention held?
   a. 1787
   b. 1776
   c. 1777
   d. 1783

Reading and Writing Exercises

The following vocabulary words will be tested on the exam. The words will be spoken out loud to you by the interviewer, and you will need to write them down on a piece of paper. Practice **writing** each sentence below, making sure you know how to spell each word correctly.

The following vocabulary words will be tested on the exam. The words will be written down on a piece of paper, and you will be asked to read them out loud to the interviewer during the exam. Practice **reading** each sentence below out loud, making sure you can pronounce all words correctly.

WRITING VOCABULARY

Washington	Adams
Father of Our Country	second
right	the
Independence Day	is
first	was
president	
July	

READING VOCABULARY

George Washington	the
Father of Our Country	was
who	is
Independence Day	of
first	president
second	country
what	

Washington was the first president.

_____

Washington is the Father of our country.

_____

Adams was the second president.

_____

Who was the first president?

Who was the Father of our country?

What is the name of the Father of our country?

George Washington was the first president.

Who was the second president?

8 ▶ THE CIVIL WAR AND MODERN HISTORY

After the Constitution was written, the country expanded in size. In 1803, the United States became much larger when it purchased **the Louisiana Territory** from France. As the country grew and added more states to the union, tensions grew between the states of the south, which owned slaves who had been sold to them from Africa, and the north, which had made **slavery** illegal. In 1861, some states of the south decided to **secede** and leave the union to start their own country. This caused the **Civil War**, which was fought from 1861–1865 between the northern and southern states. **Abraham Lincoln** was the president during the Civil War, and he wrote the **Emancipation Proclamation** to free the slaves. In 1865, the north, led by Lincoln, won the war and slavery was ended.

By the twentieth century, the United States had become a major force on the world stage. From 1917–1918, the United States fought in **World War I**. **Woodrow Wilson** was the president at this time. America's role in **World War II** established our country as a world leader. America and its allies fought against Germany, Italy, and Japan, and helped to win the war in 1945. **Franklin Delano Roosevelt (FDR)** was the president during this war. **Dwight Eisenhower**, who later became president, was a general during this war. From the 1950s–1990s, the United States participated in a **cold war** against the former Soviet Union, which was a struggle against **communism**; it also fought wars in Korea (**the Korean War**), Vietnam (**the Vietnam War**) and in the Persian Gulf (**the Persian Gulf War**).

In the 1960s, the **civil rights movement** fought for the rights of groups that had been treated unfairly. **Dr. Martin Luther King, Jr.**, fought for the equality of all Americans, and 100 years before him, **Susan B. Anthony** struggled for the rights of women.

On **September 11, 2001**, a great tragedy occurred when terrorists attacked the United States.

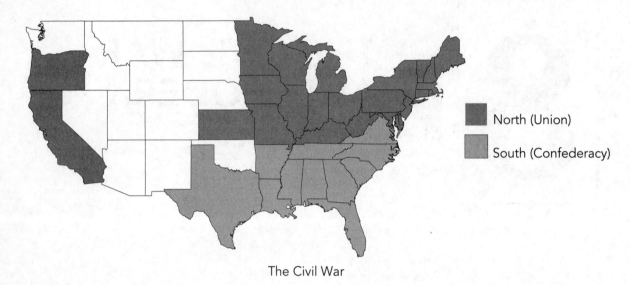

North (Union)

South (Confederacy)

The Civil War

Words to Know

Louisiana Territory: large territory the United States purchased from France in 1803

Slavery: the practice of owning other people

Secede: leave the union

Civil War: the war between the north and the south of America, from 1861–1865

Abraham Lincoln: the 16th president, who led the north to win the Civil War

Emancipation Proclamation: freed the slaves, written by Abraham Lincoln

Susan B. Anthony: a civil rights leader who fought for women's rights

Woodrow Wilson: U.S. president during World War I

World War II: a war in which America and its allies fought against Germany, Italy, and Japan

Franklin Delano Roosevelt (FDR): U.S. president during World War II

Dwight Eisenhower: general during World War II and later a president of the United States

Civil rights: equal rights for all citizens

Dr. Martin Luther King, Jr.: a civil rights leader

Persian Gulf War: a conflict to eject Iraqi forces from Kuwait in the 1990s

September 11, 2001: the date of a terrorist attack on the United States

Abraham Lincoln

Related Questions

1. **Q:** Name the wars the United States fought during the 1800s.
A: The United States fought the **Civil War**, the **War of 1812, Mexican-American War, Spanish-American War.**

2. **Q:** What continent did the slaves come from?
A: The slaves came from **Africa.**

3. **Q:** What is one important thing Abraham Lincoln did as president?
A: Abraham Lincoln **led the United States during the Civil War, freed the slaves,** and **preserved the union.**

4. **Q:** What did the Emancipation Proclamation do?
A: The Emancipation Proclamation **freed the slaves in the south.**

5. **Q:** What was the war that was fought between the northern and southern states?
A: The **Civil War** was fought between the northern and southern states.

6. **Q:** Who was Susan B. Anthony and what did she do?
A: Susan B. Anthony was **a civil rights leader who fought for women's rights.**

7. **Q:** What did Dr. Martin Luther King, Jr., do?
A: Martin Luther King, Jr., **fought for equal rights for all Americans.**

8. **Q:** Who was our president during World War I?
A: **Woodrow Wilson** was president during World War I.

9. **Q:** Before he was president, Eisenhower was a general. During what war was he a general?
A: Eisenhower was a general during **World War II.**

10. **Q:** What was the United States fighting against during the Cold War?
A: The United States fought against **communism** during the Cold War.

11. **Q:** What movement sought to end discrimination and provide rights for everyone?
A: The **civil rights movement** sought to end discrimination and provide rights for everyone.

12. **Q:** What happened on September 11, 2001?
A: Terrorists attacked the United States on September 11, 2001.

13. **Q:** Name one problem that led to the Civil War.
A: Slavery, economic reasons, and states' rights led to the Civil War.

14. **Q:** Name one war fought by the United States in the 1900s.
A: The United States fought World War I, World War II, the Korean War, the Vietnam War, and the (Persian) Gulf War.

15. **Q:** Who was the president during the Great Depression and World War II?
A: Franklin Roosevelt

16. **Q:** Who did the United States fight in World War II?
A: The United States fought Japan, Germany, and Italy during World War II.

Dr. Martin Luther King, Jr.

Exercises

Fill in the Blank

The answers to these seven questions can be found on page 97.

1. The United States purchased _____ from France in 1803.

2. In _____, the northern states of the United States fought against the southern states and won.

3. A primary reason for the Civil War was _____.

4. Abraham Lincoln's _____ freed the slaves.

5. The president of the United States during World War II was _____.

6. The _____ movement worked to end discrimination.

7. On September 11, 2001, _____ attacked the United States.

Multiple Choice

Choose the best answer for each question. Answers can be found on page 97.

1. Civil rights means
   a. that citizens must be polite to one another.
   b. equal rights for all citizens.
   c. the ability to leave the union.
   d. the right to bear arms.

2. Who was the president during World War I?
   a. Woodrow Wilson
   b. Thomas Jefferson
   c. James Madison
   d. Dwight Eisenhower

3. The Cold War describes a struggle between the U.S. and which other country?
   a. Italy
   b. Great Britain
   c. Soviet Union
   d. France

Reading and Writing Exercises

The following vocabulary words will be tested on the exam. The words will be spoken out loud to you by the interviewer, and you will need to write them down on a piece of paper. Practice **writing** each sentence below, making sure you know how to spell each word correctly.

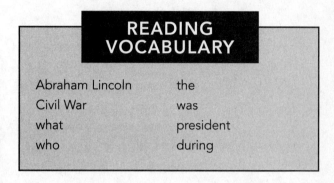

WRITING VOCABULARY

Lincoln	the
Civil War	was
president	a
during	

Lincoln was President during the Civil War.

_____

Lincoln was a president.

_____

The following vocabulary words will be tested on the exam. The words will be written down on a piece of paper, and you will be asked to read them out loud to the interviewer during the exam. Practice **reading** each sentence below out loud, making sure you can pronounce all words correctly.

READING VOCABULARY

Abraham Lincoln	the
Civil War	was
what	president
who	during

Who was Abraham Lincoln?

What was the Civil War?

Who was president during the Civil War?

THE U.S. GOVERNMENT

The U.S. government follows a system of checks and balances, with each of the three branches of government balancing the others. First, we will review the Constitution, which is the foundation of American government and laws. Next, we will examine each of the three branches of government.

Here is a chart to help you sort out the three branches of government at the various levels:

	LEGISLATIVE		**EXECUTIVE**	**JUDICIAL**
Federal Government	House of Representatives	Senate	president, vice president, cabinet	Supreme Court (justices)
State Government	State House of Representatives	State Senate	governor	State Supreme Court
Municipal (City) Government	city council		mayor	municipal court

LESSON 9 ▶ THE CONSTITUTION

The **Constitution** is the supreme law of the land. It was written at the Constitutional Convention in 1787, after the Americans won their freedom from Great Britain. It defined the branches of government and established a structure for the new nation of America. The **Preamble**, or introduction to the Constitution, begins with the words, "We the people of the United States."

The supreme law of the land also allows for changes to the Constitution itself, which are called **amendments**. Since 1787, 27 amendments to the Constitution have been passed. The first ten amendments are called the **Bill of Rights**. They were passed immediately to guarantee the rights and freedoms to all people in America. These rights include **freedom of speech**, **press**, **religion**, **expression**, **assembly**, **freedom to petition the government**, and **the right to bear arms**.

The Constitution sets up the **rule of law**, the idea that no one is above the law and that leaders and the government must follow the same law as everyone else.

Furthermore, the Constitution sets up the structure of the government, dividing it into the **legislative branch**, the **executive branch**, and the **judicial branch**. It divides power between the **federal government**, or government at the national level, and state and local governments. The federal government has certain important powers, including the power to print money and to sign treaties. State and city governments have other jobs, including providing education and providing police and fire departments. It also lists the basic rights that everyone has.

The Constitution

Words to Know

Constitution: the supreme law of the land
Preamble: the introduction to the Constitution
Amendments: changes to the Constitution
Bill of Rights: the first ten amendments
Rule of law: the idea that the government must follow the law and that no one is above the law
Federal government: government at the national level, consisting of the legislative, executive, and judicial branches

Related Questions

1. **Q:** What does the Constitution do?
    A: The Constitution **sets up the government**, **protects the basic rights of Americans**, and **establishes the rule of law.**

2. **Q:** What is the supreme law of the United States?
    A: **The Constitution** is the supreme law of the United States.

3. **Q:** In what year was the Constitution written?
    A: The Constitution was written in **1787**.

4. **Q:** What is the introduction to the Constitution called?
    A: The introduction to the Constitution is called **the Preamble**.

5. **Q:** The idea of self-government is in the first three words of the Constitution. What are these words?
    A: "We the People."

6. **Q:** What is an amendment?
    A: An amendment is a **change or addition to the Constitution**.

7. **Q:** How many amendments does the Constitution have?
    A: The Constitution has **27 amendments**.

8. **Q:** What are first ten amendments called?
    A: The first ten amendments are called the **Bill of Rights**.

9. **Q:** What does freedom of religion mean?
    A: Freedom of religion means **the right to practice any religion or no religion at all**.

10. **Q:** Name three rights or freedoms guaranteed by the Bill of Rights.
A: Three rights or freedoms guaranteed by the Bill of Rights are **freedom of speech**, **freedom of press**, and **freedom of religion**.

11. **Q:** Whose rights are guaranteed by the Constitution and the Bill of Rights?
A: The rights of **all people in America** are guaranteed by the Constitution.

12. **Q:** What is the idea behind the rule of law?
A: The rule of law says that **no one is above the law and everyone must obey it**.

13. **Q:** Name the three branches of government.
A: The three branches of government are **legislative**, **executive**, and **judicial**.

14. **Q:** What is a power the federal government has under the Constitution?
A: The federal government can **print money**, **declare war**, **create an army**, and **make treaties**.

15. **Q:** What is one power of a state government?
A: The state government can **provide education**, **police and fire departments**, and **issue driver's licenses**.

16. **Q:** What is one right or freedom from the 1st amendment?
A: Freedom of speech, religion, assembly, press, and freedom to petition the government.

17. **Q:** What happened at the Constitutional Convention?
A: The U.S. Constitution was written, the Founding Fathers wrote the U.S. Constitution.

18. **Q:** What are two rights of everyone living in the United States?
A: Freedom of speech, expression, assembly, to petition the government, religion, and the right to bear arms.

Exercises

Fill in the Blank

The answers to these six questions can be found on page 97.

1. The _____ is the supreme law of the land.

2. The _____ is the introduction to the Constitution.

3. There have been 27 _____ to the Constitution.

4. The first ten amendments are called the _____.

5. Freedom of _____ is guaranteed by one of the ten amendments.

6. "_____" are the first three words of the Constitution.

Reading and Writing Exercises

The following vocabulary words will be tested on the exam. The words will be spoken out loud to you by the interviewer, and you will need to write them down on a piece of paper. Practice **writing** each sentence below, making sure you know how to spell each word correctly.

The Bill of Rights

WRITING VOCABULARY

freedom of speech	a
people	right
come	be
free	one
America	to
is	

Freedom of speech is one right.

_____

Freedom of speech is a right.

_____

People come to America to be free.

_____

The following vocabulary words will be tested on the exam. The words will be written down on a piece of paper, and you will be asked to read them out loud to the interviewer during the exam. Practice **reading** each sentence below out loud, making sure you can pronounce all words correctly.

READING VOCABULARY

Bill of Rights	right
government	why
what	people
is	America
one	the

What is one right?

Why do people come to America?

What is the Bill of Rights?

10 ▶ THE LEGISLATIVE BRANCH

The **legislative branch** of government makes the laws. At the federal level, the legislative branch is **Congress**, which makes the federal laws and also has the power to declare war. Congress is made up of the **Senate** and the **House of Representatives**, and its members are elected directly by the people. Both halves of Congress meet in the **U.S. Capitol** building in **Washington, D.C.**

The Capitol

The **Senate** is the smaller group, with 100 **senators**, two from each of the 50 states. Senators are elected for six-year terms. The vice president presides over the Senate. The larger **House of Representatives** has 435 **representatives**, who are elected for two-year terms. The number of representatives for each state is determined by the total population of each state and each state must have at least one representative. The Speaker of the House presides over the House of Representatives. There is no limit to the number of times a senator or representative may be reelected.

Senators

California

Rhode Island

Representatives

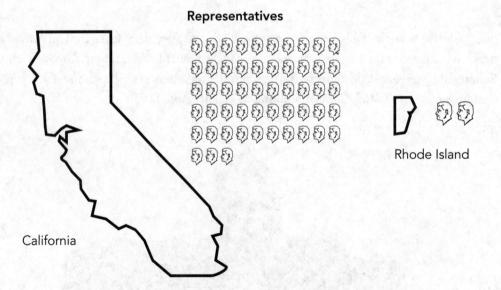

California

Rhode Island

Words to Know

Legislative branch: the branch of government that makes laws

Congress: the legislative branch of government at the federal level

Senate: one of the groups that make up Congress; has 100 members

House of Representatives: one of the groups that make up Congress; has 435 members

U.S. Capitol: a building in Washington, D.C., where Congress meets

Senator: a member of Senate

Representative: a member of the House of Representatives

Related Questions

1. **Q:** At the federal level, what is the legislative branch of government?
   A: The legislative branch at the federal level is **Congress**.

2. **Q:** Who makes the federal laws in the United States?
   A: Congress makes the federal laws.

3. **Q:** What are the two parts of Congress?
   A: The **Senate** and **the House of Representatives** are the two parts of Congress.

4. **Q:** What group has the power to declare war?
   A: Congress has the power to declare war.

5. **Q:** Who elects members of Congress?
   A: The people directly elect members of Congress.

6. **Q:** Who is one of your state's senators?
   A: My state's senator is _____.
   (Look up your state's senators.)

7. **Q:** How many senators are there in Congress?
   A: There are **100** senators in Congress.

8. **Q:** Who does a state senator represent in Congress?
   A: The state senator **represents all the people of his or her state**.

9. **Q:** For how long do we elect each senator?
   A: We elect senators for **six-year terms**.

10. **Q:** How many times may a senator or representative be reelected?
    A: There is no limit to the number of times a senator or representative may be reelected.

11. **Q:** How many representatives are in the House of Representatives?
    A: The House of Representatives has **435 representatives**.

12. **Q:** For how long do we elect representatives?
    A: We elect representatives for **two-year terms**.

13. **Q:** Where does Congress meet?
    A: Congress meets **in the U.S. Capitol building in Washington, D.C.**

14. **Q:** : Name your U.S. representative.
    A: My U.S. representative is _____.
    (Look up your U.S. representative.)

15. **Q:** Why do some states have more U.S. representatives than others?
    A: States that have **more people** have more representatives.

Exercises

Fill in the Blank

The answers to these six questions can be found on page 98.

1. Congress is made up of the _____ and the _____.

2. Only _____ has the power to declare war.

3. Congress meets in the U.S. _____ building.

4. We elect each _____ for two-year terms.

5. There is no limit to how many _____ a senator or representative may serve.

6. States with larger populations have _____ U.S. representatives.

Reading and Writing Exercises

The following vocabulary words will be tested on the exam. The words will be spoken out loud to you by the interviewer, and you will need to write them down on a piece of paper. Practice **writing** each sentence below, making sure you know how to spell each word correctly.

WRITING VOCABULARY	
congress	Washington D.C.
senators	meet
elect	we
one hundred	have
100	in
people	U.S.

We have 100/one hundred senators.

_____

We elect U.S. senators.

_____

The people elect congress.

_____

Congress meets in Washington D.C.

_____

The following vocabulary words will be tested on the exam. The words will be written down on a piece of paper, and you will be asked to read them out loud to the interviewer during the exam. Practice **reading** each sentence opposite out loud, making sure you can pronounce all words correctly.

READING VOCABULARY

congress	do
senators	we
elects	many
meet	have
how	U.S.
who	United States
does	

How many senators do we have?

We elect 100/one hundred United States Senators.

Who elects U.S. senators?

Where does congress meet?

11 ▶ THE EXECUTIVE BRANCH

The duty of the **executive branch** is to enforce the laws. At the federal level, the executive branch is the **president**, the **vice president**, the **cabinet**, and the departments under the cabinet members. The president signs bills into law and serves as **commander in chief** of the U.S. military. The cabinet is the special group that advises the president. The cabinet is made up of the following positions: **Secretary of** Agriculture, Commerce, Defense, Education, Energy, Health and Human Services, Homeland Security, Housing and Urban Development, Interior, Labor, State, Transportation, Treasury, Veterans Affairs, the Attorney General, and the Vice President. The president's official home is the **White House**, which is in Washington, D.C.

As you remember from Lesson 1, we vote for the president in November, and the new president takes office in January. In order to run for President, the candidate must be a natural-born citizen, meaning he or she was born in the United States. The president is elected to a four-year term and may only serve two full terms. The Constitution also specifies the order of presidential succession. If the president should die, the vice president would become the next president. If both the president and the vice president should die, the Speaker of the House becomes president.

At the state level, the head executive is called a **governor**.

The White House

Words to Know

Executive branch: the branch of government that enforces the laws

President: head executive at the federal level

Vice president: second in command at the federal level

Cabinet: special group that advises the president

Commander in chief: head executive of the military

White House: the president's official home

Natural-born citizen: citizen by birth in the United States

Governor: head executive at the state level

Related Questions

1. **Q:** What is the executive branch?
   A: The executive branch is **the president, the vice president, the cabinet,** and **the departments under the cabinet members**.

2. **Q:** What is the job of the cabinet?
   A: The cabinet **advises the president**.

3. **Q:** Which branch enforces laws?
   A: The **executive branch** enforces laws.

4. **Q:** Who signs bills into laws and vetoes bills?
   A: The president signs bills into laws and vetoes bills.

5. **Q:** Who is the commander in chief of the U.S. military?
   A: The president is the commander in chief of the U.S. military.

6. **Q:** How many full terms can a president serve?
   A: A president can serve **two full terms**.

7. **Q:** Who becomes president of the United States if the president should die?
   A: The vice president becomes president if the president should die.

8. **Q:** Who is the vice president of the United States today?
   A: The current vice president is **Mike Pence**.

9. **Q:** Who is the president of the United States today?
   A: The current president is **Donald Trump**.

The president leads the country

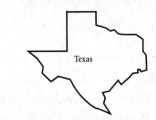

Texas

The governor leads the state

10. Q: What is the political party of the president today?
A: The current president is a member of the **Republican Party**.

11. Q: Who becomes president of the United States if both the president and the vice president should die?
A: The Speaker of the House would become president.

12. Q: Who is the Speaker of the House today?
A: Paul Ryan is the current Speaker of the House.

13. Q: For how long do we elect the president?
A: We elect the president for **four-year terms**.

14. Q: What is the White House?
A: The White House is **the president's official home**.

15. Q: During what month do we have elections for president?
A: We have elections in **November**.

16. Q: What is the head executive of a state government called?
A: The head executive of a state government is called a **governor**.

17. Q: Who is the governor of your state today?
A: The governor of my state is _____. (Look up your state's governor.)

18. Q: Who elects the president of the United States?
A: The Electoral College elects of the president of the United States.

19. Q: In what month is the new president inaugurated?
A: The new president is inaugurated in **January**.

20. Q: Who was the first president of the United States?
A: George Washington was the first president of the United States.

21. **Q:** Who was president during the Civil War?
A: Abraham Lincoln was president during the Civil War.

22. **Q:** Which president was the first commander in chief?
A: George Washington was the first commander in chief.

23. **Q:** Name two cabinet-level positions.
A: Secretary of: Agriculture, Commerce, Defense, Education, Energy, Health and Human Services, Homeland Security, Housing and Urban Development, Interior, Labor, State, Transportation, Treasury, Veterans Affairs, the Attorney General, and the Vice President.

Exercises

Fill in the Blank

The answers to these five questions can be found on page 98.

1. The _____ is the special group that advises the president.

2. The president is _____ of the U.S. military.

3. The _____ is the president's official home.

4. People vote for the president in _____.

5. The _____ elects the president.

Multiple Choice

Choose the best answer for each question. Answers can be found on page 98.

1. How many terms is the president allowed to serve?
   a. four terms
   b. two terms
   c. one term
   d. unlimited terms.

2. In which month is the president inaugurated?
   a. January
   b. November
   c. July
   d. December

3. What does a governor do?
   a. leads a state
   b. serves as a member of the president's cabinet
   c. leads a city
   d. serves in congress

Reading and Writing Exercises

The following vocabulary words will be tested on the exam. The words will be spoken out loud to you by the interviewer, and you will need to write them down on a piece of paper. Practice **writing** each sentence below, making sure you know how to spell each word correctly.

The following vocabulary words will be tested on the exam. The words will be written down on a piece of paper, and you will be asked to read them out loud to the interviewer during the exam. Practice **reading** each sentence below out loud, making sure you can pronounce all words correctly.

WRITING VOCABULARY

president	in
White House	and
lives	was
Washington D.C.	the
Adams	on
Lincoln	second
dollar bill	were
Washington	

READING VOCABULARY

president	what
White House	was
lives	where
lived	the
dollar bill	is
George Washington	on
second	in
who	does
where	

The president lives in the White House.

_____

The president lives in Washington D.C.

_____

Adams, Lincoln, and Washington were presidents.

_____

Adams was the second president.

_____

Washington is on the dollar bill.

_____

Who lives in the White House?

Where does the president live?

Who was the second president?

What president is on the dollar bill?

Who was George Washington?

12 ▶ THE JUDICIAL BRANCH

The **judicial branch** of the government interprets and explains the laws that Congress makes and the president enforces. At the federal level, the judicial branch is the **Supreme Court**, the highest court in the United States. The nine **Supreme Court justices** serve for life. The **chief justice** of the Supreme Court is the head justice. When there are openings on the Supreme Court, the president selects new Supreme Court justices.

Supreme Court

Words to Know

Judicial branch: the branch of government that interprets and explains the laws

Supreme Court: the highest court in the United States

Supreme Court justice: one of the nine judges on the Supreme Court

Chief justice: the head justice on the Supreme Court

Related Questions

1. **Q:** What does the judicial branch do?
A: The judicial branch reviews and interprets laws, resolves disputes, and determines if laws go against the Constitution.

2. **Q:** Who is the chief justice of the Supreme Court today?
A: John Roberts is the current chief justice of the Supreme Court.

3. **Q:** What is the highest court in the United States?
A: The Supreme Court is the highest court in the United States.

4. **Q:** Who selects the Supreme Court justices?
A: The president selects the Supreme Court justices.

5. **Q:** How many Supreme Court justices are there?
A: There are **nine** Supreme Court justices.

Exercises

Fill in the Blank

The answers to these five questions can be found on page 98.

1. The _____ is the highest court in America.

2. The _____ is the branch of government that interprets the laws.

3. There are _____ Supreme Court justices.

4. The Supreme Court justices are appointed by _____.

5. Supreme Court justices serve for _____.

SECTION REVIEW ▶

The section review contains a useful list of important names and concepts that were covered in Section II. The lesson number of each concept is in parentheses

    Following the review list is the official list of 100 questions, from which the interviewer at your citzenship interview will choose 10 to ask you. You will only be asked questions from the official list of 100. You should study these questions thoroughly after working through all of the exercises in Section II.

    At the end of this review you will find the answer key, which lists all of the answers to the exercises in this book and the official 100 questions.

STUDY AID

Here's a fun and effective study idea. Create flash cards to help you learn the official USCIS questions and answers. It's simple:

1. Buy index cards at your local paper goods or drug store.
2. Write a USCIS question on one side of each card and the correct answer on the back.
3. Shuffle the cards and have a friend or family member ask you the questions.
4. Keep trying until you get all of them right!

PEOPLE

Abraham Lincoln (8)	Mike Pence (11)	Permanent resident (1)
American Indians (6)	Martin Luther King, Jr. (8)	Pilgrims (6)
Donald Trump (11)	Native Americans (6)	Speaker of the House (10)
Colonists (6)	Natural-born citizen (1)	Thomas Jefferson (7)
Franklin D. Roosevelt (8)	Naturalized citizen (1)	Woodrow Wilson (8)
George Washington (7)	Paul Ryan (11)	Terrorists (8)

PLACES / DATES / WARS

PLACES	DATES	WARS
Canada (4)	July 4, 1776 (7)	American Revolution (7)
Great Britain (7)	1787 (9)	Civil War (8)
Louisiana territory (8)	1861–1865 (8)	Cold War (8)
Mexico (4)		Korean War (8)
Missouri River (4)		Persian Gulf War (8)
Mississippi River (4)		Vietnam War (8)
United States of America (1)		World War I (8)
U.S. Capitol building (10)		World War II (8)
U.S. Territories (4)		
Washington, D.C. (3)		

IDEAS / DOCUMENTS / OTHER IMPORTANT HISTORY AND EVENTS

IDEAS	DOCUMENTS	OTHER IMPORTANT HISTORY AND EVENTS
All men are created equal (8)	Amendments (9)	13 original colonies (6)
Checks and balances (3)	Bill of Rights (9)	50 states (2)
Religious freedom (6)	Constitution (9)	Civil rights movement (8)
Right to vote (1)	Declaration of Independence (7)	Independence Day (5)
Rule of law (9)	Emancipation Proclamation (8)	National holiday (5)
Speech, press, religion (9)	Federalist papers (7)	Slavery (8)
	N-400 (1)	Thanksgiving (5)
	Passport (1)	"The Star-Spangled Banner" (2)

GOVERNMENT

Cabinet (11)	Governor (11)	Minimum voting age (1)
Commander in chief (11)	House of Representatives (10)	President (11)
Congress (10)	Judicial branch (12)	Republican (1)
Democrat (1)	Justices (12)	Senate (10)
Democratic Republic (3)	Legislative (10)	Supreme Court (12)
Electoral College (1)	Limit (10)	USCIS (1)
		Vice president (11)

The 100 Questions

The following is a list of the official USCIS civics and history questions. At your interview, you will be asked 10 questions from this list and you must answer at least six of them correctly.

There is an exception—applicants who are 65 years of age or older and have been legal permanent residents of the United States for at least 20 years are only tested on a subset of the questions. Those questions are marked on this list with an asterisk (*).

AMERICAN GOVERNMENT
A: Principles of American Democracy

1. What is the supreme law of the land?

2. What does the Constitution do?

3. The idea of self-government is in the first three words of the Constitution. What are these words?

4. What is an amendment?

5. What do we call the first ten amendments to the Constitution?

6. What is one right or freedom from the First Amendment?*

7. How many amendments does the Constitution have?

8. What did the Declaration of Independence do?

9. What are two rights in the Declaration of Independence?

10. What is freedom of religion?

11. What is the economic system in the United States?*

12. What is the "rule of law"?

B: System of Government

13. Name one branch or part of the government.*

14. What stops one branch of government from becoming too powerful?

15. Who is in charge of the executive branch?

16. Who makes federal laws?

17. What are the two parts of the U.S. Congress?*

18. How many U.S. senators are there?

19. We elect a U.S. senator for how many years?

20. Who is one of your state's U.S. senators now?*

21. The House of Representatives has how many voting members?

22. We elect a U.S. representative for how many years?

23. Who is one of your state's U.S. representatives?

24. Who does a U.S. senator represent?

25. Why do some states have more representatives than other states?

26. We elect a president for how many years?

27. In what month do we vote for president?*

28. What is the name of the president of the United States now?*

29. What is the name of the vice president of the United States now?

30. If the president can no longer serve, who becomes president?

31. If both the president and the vice president can no longer serve, who becomes president?

32. Who is the commander in chief of the military?

33. Who signs bills to become laws?

34. Who vetoes bills?

35. What does the president's cabinet do?

36. What are two cabinet-level positions?

37. What does the judicial branch do?

38. What is the highest court in the United States?

39. How many justices are on the Supreme Court?

40. Who is the chief justice of the United States now?

41. Under our Constitution, some powers belong to the federal government. What is one power of the federal government?

42. Under our Constitution, some powers belong to the states. What is one power of the states?

43. Who is the governor of your state now?

44. What is the capital of your state?*

45. What are the two major political parties in the United States?*

46. What is the political party of the president now?

47. What is the name of the speaker of the House of Representatives now?

C: Rights and Responsibilities

48. There are four amendments to the Constitution about who can vote. Describe one of them.

49. What is one responsibility that is only for United States citizens?*

50. Name one right only for United States citizens.

51. What are two rights of everyone living in the United States?

52. What do we show loyalty to when we say the Pledge of Allegiance?

53. What is one promise you make when you become a United States citizen?

54. How old do citizens have to be to vote for president?*

55. What are two ways that Americans can participate in their democracy?

56. When is the last day you can send in federal income tax forms?*

57. When must all men register for the Selective Service?

AMERICAN HISTORY
A: Colonial Period and Independence

58. What is one reason colonists came to America?

59. Who lived in America before the Europeans arrived?

60. What group of people was taken to America and sold as slaves?

61. Why did the colonists fight the British?

62. Who wrote the Declaration of Independence?

63. When was the Declaration of Independence adopted?

64. There were 13 original states. Name three.

65. What happened at the Constitutional Convention?

66. When was the Constitution written?

67. The Federalist Papers supported the passage of the U.S. Constitution. Name one of the writers.

68. What is one thing Benjamin Franklin is famous for?

69. Who is the "Father of Our Country"?

70. Who was the first President?*

B: 1800s

71. What territory did the United States buy from France in 1803?

72. Name one war fought by the United States in the 1800s.

73. Name the U.S. war between the north and the south.

74. Name one problem that led to the Civil War.

75. What was one important thing that Abraham Lincoln did?*

76. What did the Emancipation Proclamation do?

77. What did Susan B. Anthony do?

C: Recent American History and Other Important Historical Information

78. Name one war fought by the United States in the 1900s.*

79. Who was President during World War I?

80. Who was President during the Great Depression and World War II?

81. Who did the United States fight in World War II?

82. Before he was President, Eisenhower was a general. What war was he in?

83. During the Cold War, what was the main concern of the United States?

84. What movement tried to end racial discrimination?

85. What did Martin Luther King, Jr. do?*

86. What major event happened on September 11, 2001, in the United States?

87. Name one American Indian tribe in the United States.

INTEGRATED CIVICS

A: Geography

88. Name one of the two longest rivers in the United States.

89. What ocean is on the West Coast of the United States?

90. What ocean is on the East Coast of the United States?

91. Name one U.S. territory.

92. Name one state that borders Canada.

93. Name one state that borders Mexico.

94. What is the capital of the United States?*

95. Where is the Statue of Liberty?*

B: Symbols

96. Why does the flag have 13 stripes?

97. Why does the flag have 50 stars?*

98. What is the name of the national anthem?

C: Holidays

99. When do we celebrate Independence Day?*

100. Name two national U.S. holidays.

Answers

Lesson 1
Fill in the Blank

1. The president of the United States is elected in November.
2. You must be at least 18 years old to vote in the United States.
3. The two major political parties in America are the Democratic and the Republican parties.
4. The right to vote is the most important right granted to American citizens.
5. Congress is directly elected by the people.

Multiple Choice

1. c
2. a
3. c

Lesson 2
Fill in the Blank

1. The colors of the flag are red, white, and blue.
2. The stars on the flag represent the 50 states in the union.
3. The stripes on the flag represent the 13 original colonies.
4. Our national anthem is called "The Star-Spangled Banner."

Multiple Choice

1. b
2. d
3. b

Lesson 3
Fill in the Blank

1. A system of checks and balances keeps any one branch of government from becoming too powerful.
2. The legislative branch of government makes the federal laws.
3. Washington, D.C. is the capital of the United States of America.
4. The system of government of the United States in which citizens elect representatives to govern them is a democratic republic.
5. The president, the vice president, and the cabinet make up the executive branch.

Multiple Choice

1. c
2. c
3. d

Lesson 4
Fill in the Blank

1. The United States is bordered by Canada to the north and Mexico to the south.
2. Guam and Puerto Rico are examples of United States territories.
3. The Mississippi and the Missouri are the country's two longest rivers.
4. Minnesota is a state that borders Canada.
5. California is a state that borders Mexico.

Multiple Choice

1. b
2. c
3. b

Lesson 5
Fill in the Blank

1. The important holiday on July 4 is Independence Day.
2. Thanksgiving, Veterans Day, and Memorial Day are all examples of national holidays.

Lesson 6
Fill in the Blank

1. The <u>pilgrims</u> were the first American colonists.
2. The 13 original states were called <u>colonies</u>.
3. The <u>Native Americans (American Indians)</u> lived in America before the colonists arrived.
4. <u>Thanksgiving</u> is the holiday that was first celebrated by the American colonists.
5. The pilgrims came to America for <u>religious freedom</u>.

Lesson 7
Fill in the Blank

1. The Declaration of Independence was adopted on <u>July 4, 1776</u>.
2. Alexander Hamilton and John Jay were two of the writers of <u>the Federalist Papers</u>.
3. The oldest member of the Constitutional Convention was <u>Benjamin Franklin</u>.
4. <u>The main writer of the Declaration of Independence was Thomas Jefferson</u>.
5. <u>George Washington</u> was the first commander in chief of the U.S. Army.
6. One of the main beliefs of the <u>Declaration of Independence</u> is that all men are created equal.

Multiple Choice

1. c
2. b
3. a

Lesson 8
Fill in the Blank

1. The United States purchased the <u>Louisiana Territory</u> from France in 1803.
2. In <u>the Civil War</u>, the northern states of the United States fought against the southern states and won.
3. The primary reason for the Civil War was <u>slavery</u>.
4. Abraham Lincoln's <u>Emancipation Proclamation</u> freed the slaves.
5. The president of the United States during World War II was <u>Franklin Delano Roosevelt (FDR)</u>.
6. The <u>civil rights</u> movement worked to end discrimination.
7. On September 11, 2001, <u>terrorists</u> attacked the United States.

Multiple Choice

1. b
2. a
3. c

Lesson 9
Fill in the Blank

1. The <u>Constitution</u> is the supreme law of the land.
2. The <u>Preamble</u> is the introduction to the Constitution.
3. There have been 27 <u>amendments</u> to the Constitution.
4. The first ten amendments are called the <u>Bill of Rights</u>.
5. Freedom of <u>speech / press / religion</u> is guaranteed by one of the ten amendments.
6. "<u>We the people</u>" are the first three words of the Constitution.

Lesson 10
Fill in the Blank

1. Congress is made up of the <u>Senate</u> and the <u>House of Representatives</u>.
2. Only <u>Congress</u> has the power to declare war.
3. Congress meets in the U.S. <u>Capitol</u> building.
4. We elect each <u>representative</u> for two-year terms.
5. There is <u>no limit</u> to how many <u>terms</u> a senator or representative may serve.
6. States with larger populations have <u>more</u> U.S. representatives.

Lesson 11
Fill in the Blank

1. The <u>cabinet</u> is the special group that advises the president.
2. The president is <u>commander in chief</u> of the U.S. military.
3. The <u>White House</u> is the president's official home.
4. People vote for the president in <u>November</u>.
5. The <u>Electoral College</u> elects the president.

Multiple Choice

1. b
2. a
3. a

Lesson 12
Fill in the Blank

1. The <u>Supreme Court</u> is the highest court in America.
2. The <u>judicial branch</u> is the branch of government that interprets the laws.
3. There are <u>nine</u> Supreme Court justices.
4. The Supreme Court justices are appointed by <u>the president</u>.
5. Supreme Court justices serve for <u>life</u>.

Answers to the 100 Questions

1. The Constitution
2. Possible answers:
   - sets up the government
   - defines the government
   - protects basic rights of Americans
3. We the People
4. A change or an addition (to the Constitution)
5. The Bill of Rights
6. Possible answers:
   - religion
   - assembly
   - press
   - petition the government
   - speech
7. Twenty-seven (27)
8. Announced our independence (from Great Britain); declared our independence (from Great Britain); OR said that the United States is free (from Great Britain)
9. Possible answers:
   - life
   - liberty
   - pursuit of happiness
10. You can practice any religion, or not practice a religion.
11. Capitalist economy or market economy
12. Possible variations:
    - Everyone must follow the law.
    - Leaders must obey the law.
    - Government must obey the law.
    - No one is above the law.
13. Possible answers:
    - Congress
    - legislative
    - president
    - executive
    - the courts
    - judicial

14. Checks and balances or separation of powers
15. The President
16. Possible answers:
    - Congress
    - Senate and House of Representatives
    - (U.S. or national) legislature
17. The Senate and House of Representatives
18. One hundred (100)
19. Six (6)
20. Look up your state senator
21. Four hundred thirty-five (435)
22. Two (2)
23. Look up your representative
24. All people of the state
25. Possible answers:
    - (because of) the state's population
    - (because) they have more people
    - (because) some states have more people
26. Four (4)
27. November
28. Donald Trump or President Trump
29. Mike Pence or Vice President Pence
30. The vice president
31. The speaker of the House
32. The president
33. The president
34. The president
35. Advises the president
36. Possible answers:
    - secretary of agriculture
    - secretary of commerce
    - secretary of defense
    - secretary of education
    - secretary of energy
    - secretary of health and human services
    - secretary of homeland security
    - secretary of housing and urban development
    - secretary of the interior
    - secretary of labor
    - secretary of state
    - secretary of transportation
    - secretary of the treasury
    - secretary of veterans affairs
    - attorney general
    - vice president
37. Possible variations:
    - reviews laws
    - explains laws
    - resolves disputes (disagreements)
    - decides if a law goes against the Constitution
38. The Supreme Court
39. Nine (9)
40. John Roberts or Chief Justice Roberts
41. Possible answers:
    - to print money
    - to declare war
    - to create an army
    - to make treaties
42. Possible answers:
    - provide schooling and education
    - provide protection (police)
    - provide safety (fire departments)
    - give a driver's license
    - approve zoning and land use
43. Look up your governor
44. Look up the capital of your state
45. Democratic and Republican
46. Republican
47. Paul Ryan or Speaker Ryan
48. Possible answers:
    - citizens eighteen (18) and older can vote
    - you don't have to pay a poll tax to vote
    - any citizen can vote
    - a male citizen of any race can vote
49. Possible answers:
    - serve on a jury
    - vote in a federal election
50. Run for federal office

51. Possible answers:
- freedom of expression
- freedom of speech
- freedom of assembly
- freedom to petition the government
- freedom of worship
- the right to bear arms

52. The United States or the flag

53. Possible answers:
- give up loyalty to other countries
- defend the Constitution and laws of the United States
- obey the laws of the United States
- serve in the U.S. military (if needed)
- serve the nation (if needed)
- be loyal to the United States

54. Eighteen (18) and older

55. Possible answers:
- vote
- join a political party
- help with a campaign
- join a civic group
- join a community group
- give an elected official your opinion on an issue
- call senators and representatives
- publicly support or oppose an issue or policy
- run for office
- write to a newspaper

56. April 15

57. between eighteen (18) and twenty-six (26)

58. Possible answers:
- freedom
- political liberty
- religious freedom
- economic opportunity
- practice their religion
- escape persecution

59. American Indians or Native Americans

60. people from Africa

61. Possible answers:
- because of high taxes (taxation without representation)
- because the British army stayed in their houses (boarding, quartering)
- because they didn't have self-government

62. Thomas Jefferson

63. July 4, 1776

64. Possible answers:
- Connecticut
- Delaware
- Georgia
- Maryland
- Massachusetts
- New Hampshire
- New Jersey
- New York
- North Carolina
- Pennsylvania
- Rhode Island
- South Carolina
- Virginia

65. The Constitution was written OR The Founding Fathers wrote the Constitution

66. 1787

67. Possible answers:
- Alexander Hamilton
- James Madison
- John Jay
- Publius

68. Possible answers:
- U.S. diplomat
- oldest member of the Constitutional Convention
- first Postmaster General of the United States
- writer of *Poor Richard's Almanac*
- started the first free libraries

69. George Washington

70. George Washington

71. The Louisiana Territory OR Louisiana

72. Possible answers:
- War of 1812
- Mexican-American War
- Civil War
- Spanish-American War

73. The Civil War OR the War between the States

74. Possible answers:
- slavery
- economic reasons
- states' rights

75. Possible answers:
- freed the slaves (Emancipation Proclamation)
- saved (preserved) the union
- led the United States during the Civil War

76. freed the slaves OR freed slaves in the Confederacy OR freed slaves in the Confederate states OR freed slaves in most southern states

77. fought for women's rights or civil rights

78. Possible answers:
- World War I
- World War II
- Korean War
- Vietnam War
- Persian Gulf War

79. Woodrow Wilson

80. Franklin Roosevelt

81. Japan, Germany, and Italy

82. World War II

83. communism

84. Civil Rights Movement

85. fought for civil rights and equality for all Americans

86. terrorists attacked the United States

87. Possible answers:
- Apache
- Arawak
- Blackfeet
- Cherokee
- Cheyenne
- Chippewa
- Choctaw
- Creek
- Crow
- Hopi
- Huron
- Inuit
- Iroquois
- Lakota
- Mohegan
- Navajo
- Oneida
- Pueblo
- Seminole
- Shawnee
- Sioux
- Teton

88. Missouri River and Mississippi River

89. Pacific Ocean

90. Atlantic Ocean

91. Possible answers:
- American Samoa
- Guam
- Northern Mariana Islands
- Puerto Rico
- U.S. Virgin Islands

92. Possible answers:
- Maine
- New Hampshire
- Vermont
- New York
- Pennsylvania
- Ohio
- Michigan
- Minnesota
- North Dakota
- Montana
- Idaho
- Washington
- Alaska

93. Possible answers:
  • California
  • Arizona
  • New Mexico
  • Texas

94. Washington, D.C.

95. Possible answers:
  • New York Harbor
  • Liberty Island
  • New Jersey
  • Near New York City
  • On the Hudson River

96. because there were 13 original colonies

97. because there is one star for each state OR
  because each star represents a state OR
  because there are 50 states

98. The Star-Spangled Banner

99. July 4

100. Possible answers:
  • New Year's Day
  • Martin Luther King, Jr. Day
  • Presidents' Day
  • Memorial Day
  • Independence Day
  • Labor Day
  • Columbus Day
  • Veterans Day
  • Thanksgiving
  • Christmas

SECTION

III ▶ THE INTERVIEW

The U.S. Citizenship Exam is given in the form of an interview. It is often referred to as a citizenship interview, naturalization interview, naturalization test, or citizenship exam. This section will walk you through the steps of the actual citizenship interview. Each chapter covers a different stage of the interview process. Work slowly and carefully through each lesson, and practice with all the exercises. The section review at the end of the section revisits some of the key questions.

Here's an outline of what's in this section:

Before You Begin

The key to the interview process is to understand what your interviewer is asking you. If you don't hear what he or she says, it is better to ask your interviewer to repeat the question than to guess what question was asked. Stay calm, and listen carefully to catch the important words in each question. The first word is often very important, and even one syllable can make a difference, such as this: **When were you born?** vs. **Where were you born?** The first question asks for the date of your birth, while the second question asks for the place of your birth.

Here are a few tips to keep in mind during the interview process:

- Stay calm!
- Identify the key question words: *Who, What, When, Where, Why,* and *How*
- Think carefully about your answer.
- And remember these useful phrases:
  - **Please repeat that.**
  - **Please speak more slowly.**
  - **Please speak louder.**

What to Bring to Your Interview

You should bring all of the following documents with you to your interview—both originals and a copy of each for the interviewer to keep with your records. These documents should be original or certified copies and in English. If your documents are not in English, a certified translator must translate them and they must be marked as such. Translators cannot be an interested party, friend, or family member.

- Photo identification
- Permanent resident card
- Passport
- Any travel documents issued by the USCIS
- Copies of your tax returns from the past five years
- Selective Service registration documents
- Any arrest reports, certified court dispositions, or probation reports that you might have
- If you have arranged to take an alternate Oath of Allegiance for religious reasons, you should bring supporting documents (such as a letter from your religious organization)

THE PRE-INTERVIEW

Even before your actual interview starts, the interviewer will get an idea of your English-speaking level through greetings and small talk. Be prepared to start answering questions as soon as you enter the testing room. Just before the formal interview, you will be asked to take a truth oath, and your interviewer will check your identity. This chapter will prepare you for each of these steps so that you can focus on the actual interview itself.

13 ▶ GREETINGS AND SMALL TALK

At the USCIS building, the interviewer will call your name and lead you to an office. Before starting the interview, he or she will begin with some general conversation, or small talk, to see how well you speak English. Every interviewer is different. Some interviewers will be friendly and talkative. Other interviewers will be serious and less talkative. Be prepared for many different personalities. The interviewers job is to determine whether or not you are capable of communicating properly. If the interviewer feels that he or she cannot successfully communicate with you in English, the interview may end. The interviewer must feel strongly that you understand the questions he or she asks you. Your answers are recorded, and are permanently added to your record. Therefore, it is very important to prepare! Here are some questions that the interviewer might ask you, along with sample answers.

"How Are You?" Questions

Q: How are you?
A: I am fine / good / great. OR Fine / Good, thank you.

Q: How is the weather today?
A: The weather is fine / good / cold / warm / sunny / rainy / windy. (Pick which one applies.)

Q: How did you get here today?
A: I came by car / bus / subway / train. OR My son / daughter brought me.

Why You Are Here

Q: Do you understand why you are here today?
A: Yes

Q: Why are you here today?
A: For my citizenship interview. OR Because I want to be a U.S. citizen.

Q: Why do you want to become a U.S. citizen?
A: Because I love America.
A: America is a great country and I want to be with my family.
A: America is a great country and I want to stay.
A: America is a safe country.

Beginning the Interview

Q: Do you have any questions before we begin?
A: No

Preparation and Study

Q: Have you prepared for the citizenship test?
A: Yes

Q: Have you studied for the citizenship test?
A: Yes

Q: How did you study / prepare?
A: I read a book. OR I took a class. OR My children helped me.

14 ▶ TRUTH OATH AND IDENTITY CHECK

Now the interviewer will ask you to take the truth oath. He or she will ask you to swear that you will tell the truth during the interview. This is a very serious oath. Everything that you say to the interviewer, after this oath, must be the truth. A person who lies during the citizenship interview is committing a crime, and there may be serious consequences. This is why it is so important to prepare, and make sure you understand everything that is being said to you. On the following page is the oath that you will hear at the interview. Practice these phrases out loud several times before the interview.

Interviewer: "Okay, let's begin. Please stand and raise your right hand."

What you do: Get out of your chair and put your right hand in the air.

What it means: You are getting ready to take an oath, or promise.

Interviewer: "Do you promise to tell the truth and nothing but the truth so help you God?" OR "Do you swear that everything you say today will be the truth?"

What you do: Answer out loud, "<u>Yes</u>."

What it means: You promise to tell the truth. You promise to tell no lies.

Interviewer: "Please sit down." OR "You can sit down now."

What you do: Sit down in your chair again.

What it means: The oath is finished.

The interviewer may ask you if you understand the oath, and what it means, after you have taken it. You need to be prepared to describe the oath's purpose. The following is an example of a correct answer:

Q: Do you understand what an oath is?
A: <u>Yes, it is a promise to tell the truth.</u>

The interviewer will then check your identity, and you will have to show your verification information, such as the Appointment Notice and alien registration card.

Interviewer: "At this point, I have to check your identity. I need to see your **Appointment Notice** or **Invitation to Appear**. I would also like to see your passport if you have one, and your **alien registration card**."

What you do: Show the letter you received in the mail from USCIS, which is called your **Appointment Notice** or **Invitation to Appear**. Then show your **alien registration card**.

What it means: You can prove who you are.

After the interviewer has checked your identity, the actual interview will begin.

9 ▶ THE N-400 QUESTIONS

The first part of the citizenship interview is going through your N-400 application. This part is just as important as the civics, reading, and writing portions of the interview. It is a test of English skills, as well. You will need to understand every question on the form, every answer you provided, and you will need the ability to explain your answers, when needed. (For instance, you will need to be able to discuss any criminal charges or arrests, if relevant.) Your interviewer will most likely ask you the questions using the words exactly as they appear on the N-400 form; however, it is not guaranteed. Practice the questions with family or friends using a copy of your application, before your interview date. In the event that you cannot understand a question, the interviewer may stop the interview, and ask you to practice more before returning for a second chance. Remember, you only get two chances before you must start over and reapply. Practice is very important!

Lesson 15: General Information   **113**

Key Concepts:

- Your name and information about your eligibility
- Information about you
- Marital status

15 ▶ GENERAL INFORMATION

Your interviewer will go through your N-400 form to check the information you wrote. Be sure to keep a copy of your N-400 form to review the answers to all the following questions.

N:400: General and Biographical Information

Q: What is your name?
A: My name is _____.

Q: Spell your last name.
A: __-__-__-__-__-__-__-__-__-__-__-__-__

Q: When did you first come to the United States?
A: I came to the United States on _____ (month, day, year).

Q: Have you ever used a different name?
A: <u>Yes</u> / <u>No</u>

Q: Do you want to change your name?
A: <u>Yes</u> / <u>No</u> (If yes, say what you want to change it to.)

Q: To what do you want to change your name? OR What name do you want to have now?
A: _____.

Q: What other names have you gone by? OR What other names have you used in the past?
A: _____ OR <u>None</u>.

Q: What was your maiden name?
A: Before I was married, my name was

_____.

Q: How long have you been a permanent resident of the United States? OR How long have you lived in the United States?
A: _____ years

Q: When did you become a permanent resident? OR When did you first come to the United States? OR On what date did you enter the United States?
A: _____ (month, day, year)

Q: You've been a permanent resident since _____, is that correct?
A: <u>Yes</u> (If no, say the correct date.)

Q: Where did you enter the United States? OR What was your port of entry? OR In what port of entry did you arrive in America?
A: _____.

Q: What is your date of birth? OR What is your birthday? OR When were you born?
A: I was born on _____
(month, day, year).

Q: What is your country of birth? OR Where were you born?
A: I was born in _____ (country).

Q: What is your nationality? OR What is your current citizenship?
A: I am _____ (nationality).

Q: What is your Social Security number?
NOTE: You might NOT want to write your Social Security number in this book, but it is a very good idea to memorize it.
A: My Social Security number is

— — — - — — - — — — —.

Q: What is your marital status?
A: I am <u>single</u> / <u>married</u> / <u>divorced</u> / <u>widowed</u>.

Q: Are you married?
A: <u>Yes</u> / <u>No</u>

Q: Have you ever been divorced?
A: <u>Yes</u> / <u>No</u>

Q: Was your marriage annulled?
A: <u>Yes</u> / <u>No</u>

Q: How long have you been married?
A: I have been married for _____ years.

Q: What is your home address? OR Where do you live?
A: I live at _____.

Q: What is your home phone number? OR What is your telephone number at home?
A: My phone number is

— — —-— — —-— — — —.

Q: Do you have a work telephone number?
A: <u>Yes</u> / <u>No</u> OR No, I am not currently working.

Q: What is your work phone number?
A: My work phone number is

— — —-— — —-— — — —.

Q: What is your e-mail address?
A: My e-mail address is _____.

Q: Were your parents married before your 18th birthday?
A: <u>Yes</u> / <u>No</u>

Q: What is your mother/father's name?
A: _____.

Q: What is your mother/father's country of birth
A: _____.

Q: What is your mother/father's birthday?
A: _____.

Q: When did your mother/father become a U.S. citizen?
A: _____.

Q: What is your height? OR How tall are you?
A: I am _____ feet, _____ inches tall.

Q: What is your weight? OR How much do you weigh?
A: I weigh _____ pounds.

Q: Are you Hispanic? OR Are you Latino/a?
A: <u>Yes</u> / <u>No</u>

Q: What is your race?
A: <u>I am White / Asian / Black or African American / American Indian or Alaskan Native / Native Hawaiian or Other Pacific Islander / Other: _____</u>.

Q: What is your hair color? OR What color is your hair?
A: My hair is <u>black / brown / blonde / gray / white / red / sandy / other: _____</u>. OR I am bald.

Q: What is your eye color?
A: My eyes are <u>brown / blue / green / hazel / gray / black / other: _____</u>.

16 ▶ MORE DETAILED INFORMATION

Your interviewer may ask you to answer the following questions with detailed information. Or, your interviewer may also just read off your N-400 form and ask you if that information is right. Be sure to know all the information on your N-400 form thoroughly. If your information changes after you mail in your N-400 form, be ready to explain the changes.

Information about Your Residence and Employment

Q: Where have you lived in the past five years?
A: I have lived at _____ (list all addresses beginning with your current address).

Q: Are these all the places you have lived in the last five years?
A: <u>Yes</u> / <u>No</u> (If no, explain why you did not write it on the form.)

Q: Have you lived in any other places in the last five years?
A: <u>Yes</u> / <u>No</u> (If yes, explain why you did not write it on the form.)

Q: Have you worked in the last five years?
A: Yes / No

Q: Are you currently employed? OR Do you have a job?
A: Yes / No

Q: Why aren't you working?
A: I am not working because_____.
(Be honest!)

Q: What is your occupation? OR What do you do? OR What kind of work do you do?
A: I am / was a _____. OR I am retired.

Q: Where do you work? OR Who do you work for? OR Who is your employer? OR How do you support yourself?
A: I work at _____.

Q: How long have you worked there? OR How long have you held this job?
A: I have worked there for _____ years.

Q: Who was your employer before that?
A: _____.

Q: Please list your employers in the past five years.
A: I have worked for _____

_____

_____

_____

_____

(list all employers).

Q: Is this list of employers complete?
A: Yes / No (If no, explain why you did not write it on the form.)

Time Outside the United States

Q: Since becoming a permanent resident, have you ever left the United States? OR Have you left the United States since you became a permanent resident? OR Since coming to the United States, have you traveled to any other country? OR Have you visited any other country since becoming a permanent resident?
A: Yes / No

Q: How many times have you left the United States since you became a permanent resident?
A: _____ times

Q: How long were you away?
A: I was gone for _____ days / weeks / months / years.

Q: What country did you travel to? OR Where did you go?
A: I went to _____.

Q: Why did you leave the United States?
A: I left because _____.

Q: Did any of these trips last six months or more?
A: Yes / No (If yes, be prepared to explain why.)

Q: When was your most recent trip? OR When was the last time you left the United States?
A: It was _____.

Q: For how long were you in _____ (country)?
A: I was gone for _____ days / weeks / months / years.

Information about Your Marital History

The following questions ask about your marital status. If you have never been married, you do not need to review this section. Skip to the next section on page 120.

Q: What is your marital status?
A: I am <u>single / married / divorced / widowed</u>.

Q: Have you ever been married?
A: <u>Yes</u> / <u>No</u>

Q: Are you married?
A: <u>Yes</u> / <u>No</u>

Q: How many times have you been married?
A: I have been married _____ times.

Q: What is the full name of your husband / wife?
A: My husband's / wife's name is
_____.

Q: What is your husband's / wife's date of birth?
A: __ __ / __ __ / __ __ __ __

Q: When did you marry him / her?
A: __ __ / __ __ / __ __ __ __

Q: What is his / her current address?
A: _____.

Q: Is your husband / wife a U.S. citizen?
A: <u>Yes</u> / <u>No</u>

Q: What is his / her immigration status?
A: He / she is a permanent resident. OR He / she is a U.S. citizen.

Q: What is his / her country of citizenship?
A: _____.

Q: When did he / she become a U.S. citizen?
A: __ __ / __ __ / __ __ __ __.

Q: If your husband / wife is NOT a U.S. citizen, what is his / her country of origin?
A: He / <u>she is from</u> _____.

Q: If your husband / wife is NOT a U.S. citizen, what is his / her USCIS "A" number?
A: <u>His / her USCIS "A" number is</u>
_____.

Q: Have you been married/divorced before? What is the name of your prior spouse?
A: Yes / No _____.

Q: What is the birthday of your prior spouse?
A: _____.

Q: What is the country of birth of your prior spouse?
A: _____.

Q: What is the country of citizenship of your prior spouse?
A: _____.

Q: When did you marry your prior spouse?
A: _____.

Q: When did your marriage end with your prior spouse?
A: _____.

Q: How did your marriage end with your prior spouse?
A: _____.

Q: What is the name of your current husband/ wife's prior spouse?

A: _____.

Q: What is the birthday of your current husband/ wife's prior spouse?

A: _____.

Q: What is the country of birth of your husband/ wife's prior spouse?

A: _____.

Q: What is the country of citizenship of your husband/wife's prior spouse?

A: _____.

Q: When did your husband/wife marry the prior spouse?

A: _____.

Q: When did your husband's/wife's marriage end with the prior spouse?

A: _____.

Q: How did your husband's/wife's marriage end with the prior spouse?

A: _____.

Information about Your Children

Q: How many children do you have? OR How many sons and daughters do you have?

A: _____

Q: What are the full names of your sons and daughters?

A: (Say each child's first, middle, and last name.)

Q: Do your children live with you?

A: <u>Yes</u> / <u>No</u>

Q: How many people live in your house?

A: _____ people: myself, <u>my husband / wife</u>, and _____ children.

Q: Who do you live with?

A: I live with _____.

Q: Where do your children live?

A: My children live with me in _____.

OR Other: _____.

Q: Did any of your children stay in your native country?

A: <u>Yes</u> / <u>No</u>

Q: When were your children born?

A: One was born in _____,

one in _____,

and one in _____ (or more).

Q: Were they all born in the United States?

A: <u>Yes</u> / <u>No</u>

Q: What are your children's A (Alien) numbers?

A: _____.

LESSON 17 ▶ ADDITIONAL QUESTIONS

The following questions are all yes or no questions. Pay attention to the beginning of each question, because that will give you a clue about how to answer it. However, make sure you know what each question is asking. The majority of applicants will answer "No" to the questions in this section. The questions are related to your character and honesty. They are meant to determine if you are of "Good Moral Character" and qualify to become a U.S. citizen. The "Sentence Pattern" section below is meant to help you with identifying the beginning of each question, and the correct answer. However, BE CAREFUL! Everyone is unique, and there may be questions in this section that you answer "Yes" to. You must be honest. Be prepared to answer correctly and explain yourself if you answer "Yes" to any of the questions that follow.

Also, your interviewer may phrase the question differently. Therefore, a "yes" answer may turn into a "no" answer, based on how the interviewer phrases the question. It is best to thoroughly understand each question and answer. If the interviewer believes you are not fully understanding the questions, they will end the interview and you will have to return in approximately 60 days for a second and final chance.

SENTENCE PATTERNS	
FOR QUESTIONS BEGINNING WITH:	**ANSWER:**
"Have you ever . . ."	No
"Did you ever . . ."	No
"Do you owe . . ."	No
"Do you believe . . ."	Yes
"Do you support . . ."	Yes
"If the law requires it, are you willing . . ."	Yes

General Questions

Q: **Have you ever** claimed (in writing or in any other way) to be a U.S. citizen? OR **Have you ever** pretended to be a U.S. citizen?

Q: **Have you ever** registered to vote in any federal, state, or local election in the United States? OR **Have you ever** voted in any federal, state, or local election in the United States?

Q: Since becoming a lawful permanent resident, **have you ever** failed to file a required federal, state, or local tax return? OR **Do you owe** any federal, state, or local taxes that are overdue?

Q: Do you have any title of nobility in any foreign country? OR Were you born with or have you acquired any title of nobility? OR Are you a king, queen, duke, earl, prince, or princess, or do you have any other title of nobility?

Q: **Have you ever** been declared legally incompetent or been confined to a mental institution within the last five years? OR **Have you ever** been in a mental hospital? OR **Have you ever** been confined as a patient in a mental institution?
A: <u>No</u> (If yes, explain.)

Affiliations

Q: **Have you ever** been affiliated with any organization, association, fund, foundation, party, club, or society in the United States or in any other place?

Q: What is the name of the organization?

Q: What is the purpose?

Q: When were you a member?

Q: **Have you ever** been a member of the communist party?

Q: **Have you ever** been a member of any other totalitarian party?

Q: **Have you ever** been a member of a terrorist organization?

Q: **Have you ever** advocated the overthrow of any government by force or violence?

Q: **Have you ever** persecuted any person because of race, religion, national origin, membership in a particular social group, or political opinion?

Q: **Have you ever** worked for or been associated with the Nazi government of Germany or any government in any place that was occupied by, allied with, or established with the help of the Nazi government?

Q: Were you ever involved in any way with any of the following: Genocide? Torture? Killing or hurting someone? Forcing someone to have sexual relations? Not letting someone practice their religion?

Q: Were you ever a member or did you ever help any of the following: Military unit? Paramilitary? Police? Self-defense unit? Rebel group? Vigilante group? Guerilla group? Militia? Insurgent organization?

Q: Did you ever work or volunteer in a prison? Jail? Detention facility? Labor camp?

Q: Were you ever part of a group that used weapons against another person or threatened to do so?

Q: Did you ever sell or give weapons to another person?

Q: Did you ever recruit a person under the age of 15 to serve in an armed group?
A: <u>No</u> (If yes, explain why.)

Continuous Residence

Q: Have you ever called yourself a "nonresident" on a federal, state, or local tax return?

Q: Have you ever failed to file a federal, state, or local tax return because you considered yourself to be a nonresident?
A: <u>No</u> (If yes, explain why.)

Paying Taxes

Q: Have you ever failed to file a federal income tax return?

Q: Was there ever a year when you didn't file your federal tax forms?
A: <u>No</u> (If you have failed to file taxes, say "yes" and explain why.)

Q: Have you filed your federal taxes every year?

Q: Do you pay taxes?
A: <u>Yes</u> (If you have not filed federal taxes every year, say "no" and explain why.)

Military Service

Q: Have you ever served in the U.S. Armed Forces?

Q: Have you ever left the United States to avoid being drafted into the U.S. Armed Forces? OR **Have you ever** left the United States so you didn't have to fight in a war?

Q: Have you ever applied for any kind of exemption from military service in the U.S. Armed Forces?

Q: Have you ever deserted from the U.S Armed Forces?

Q: Have you ever failed to comply with Selective Service laws?

Q: Have you ever tried to avoid military service?

Q: Have you ever been court-martialed or disciplined by the U.S. armed forces?
A: <u>No</u>

Removal, Exclusion, and Deportation Proceedings

Q: Are removal, exclusion, rescission, or deportation proceedings pending against you?

Q: **Have you ever** been removed, excluded, or deported from the United States?

Q: **Have you ever** been ordered to be removed, excluded, or deported from the United States?

Q: **Have you ever** applied for any kind of relief from removal, exclusion, or deportation?
A: <u>No</u>

LESSON 18 ▶ GOOD MORAL CHARACTER

In order to be eligible for citizenship, you must be a person of "Good Moral Character." This is a legal term, defined by immigration law. An applicant for citizenship will be found to lack good moral character if he or she has been convicted of murder, an aggravated felony, crime of moral turpitude, false testimony or perjury, many drug offenses, gambling, prostitution, and smuggling offenses, among others. The interviewer will ask you a series of questions to determine if you lack this good moral character requirement. If you are concerned about this issue, or you believe you may have to answer "yes" to any of the following questions, you may want to consider talking with an immigration attorney prior to applying for citizenship. A conviction for some of these crimes may make you ineligible for U.S. citizenship.

In the event that you must answer "yes" to any of the following questions, you must also be prepared to explain your answer in detail. For example, your interviewer may ask you what the outcome of your arrest was, if you answered "yes" to being arrested. Bring official documents related to any "yes" answers, if available, and practice describing the situation before your interview day. Most importantly, answer all questions honestly. USCIS completes thorough background checks on you prior to your interview, and interviewers have detailed information on your history. If you hide information from the interviewer, or on the application, and USCIS learns otherwise, your application may be denied and there may be criminal consequences. Honesty is the best policy!

Q: Have you ever committed a **crime** or **offense** for which you were not arrested?
A: <u>No</u>, I have never committed a crime and have never been arrested.

Q: Have you ever been **arrested**, **cited**, or **detained** by any law enforcement officer for any reason?
A: <u>No</u>, I have never been arrested, cited, or detained.

Q: Have you ever been **charged** with committing any crime or offense?
A: <u>No</u>, I have never been charged with a crime.

Q: Have you ever been **convicted** of a crime or offense?
A: <u>No</u>, I have never been convicted of a crime.

Q: Have you ever been placed in an **alternative sentencing** or a **rehabilitative program**?
A: <u>No</u>, I have not.

Q: Have you ever received a **suspended sentence**, been placed on **probation**, or been **paroled**?
A: <u>No</u>, I have not.

Q: Have you ever been in **jail** or **prison**?
A: <u>No</u>, I have never been in jail or prison.

Q: Have you ever been a **habitual drunkard**? OR Were you ever drunk every day?
A: <u>No</u>, I drink only a little. OR <u>No</u>, I don't drink alcohol.

Q: Have you ever advocated or practiced **polygamy**? OR Have you ever been married to more than one person at the same time?
A: <u>No</u>

Q: Have you ever been a **prostitute**? OR Have you ever sold your body for money?
A: <u>No</u>, I've never taken money for sex.

Q: Have you ever knowingly and for gain helped any alien to enter the United States illegally? OR Have you ever **smuggled** anyone into the United States? OR Have you ever accepted money for sneaking someone into the United States?
A: <u>No</u>, I have never helped anyone enter the United States illegally.

Q: Have you ever bought or sold **illegal drugs**? OR Have you ever been a trafficker in illegal drugs? OR Have you ever carried illegal drugs for someone else? OR Have you ever been a trafficker in cocaine or crack? OR Have you ever bought or sold marijuana or speed?
A: <u>No</u>, I have never bought or sold illegal drugs.

Q: Have you ever received income from illegal **gambling**? OR Did you ever get money illegally from gambling? OR Have you ever received money from illegal gambling? OR Have you ever received money or other goods from illegal gambling?
A: <u>No</u>, I don't gamble.

Q: Have you ever married someone to get immigration benefits?
A: <u>No</u>, I have never married just to get immigration benefits.

Q: Have you ever failed to pay child support or alimony? Support your children or dependents?
A: <u>No</u>, I always pay support/I have never failed to pay support.

Q: Have you ever lied to get public benefits such as food stamps?
A: <u>No</u>, I have not lied to get benefits.

Q: Have you ever given U.S. government workers information that was false or documents that were fraudulent?
A: <u>No</u>, I have not.

Q: Have you ever lied to any U.S. government worker to enter or stay in the United States?
A: <u>No</u>, I have never lied.

Words to Know

Habitual drunkard: person who drinks too much alcohol

Polygamy: having more than one husband or wife at the same time

Prostitute: to sell your body for money

Smuggle: illegally sneaking someone into the country

Illegal drugs: drugs that are produced, distributed and/or possessed in an unlicensed, or illegal way

Gamble: play games for money

19 ▶ OATH REQUIREMENTS

These last six questions will almost certainly be asked at your interview, because they are the requirements for the Oath of Allegiance to the United States. The answer to all of these questions should be "yes" if you want to become an American citizen, but be sure you know what each question means. Study the questions and vocabulary, and then read the full Oath of Allegiance that follows. If you pass your interview, the interviewer will ask you to read the Oath of Allegiance and sign your name. You will not be required to read the Oath out loud. The interviewer only wants you to read it to yourself, before you sign. You should become familiar with the oath prior to your interview.

Q: 1. Do you support the **Constitution** and form of government of the United States?

2. Do you understand the full **Oath of Allegiance** to the United States?

3. Are you willing to take the full Oath of Allegiance to the United States?

4. If the law requires it, are you willing to **bear arms** on behalf of the United States?

5. If the law requires it, are you willing to perform **noncombatant services** in the U.S. Armed Forces?

6. If the law requires it, are you willing to perform work of national importance under civilian direction?

A: <u>Yes</u>

There are many people in this world who do not believe in violence or using guns to harm others, even during a war. Also, many religions believe that their followers should never kill or harm another person. The United States Constitution recognizes that some people strongly believe they cannot "bear arms on behalf of the United States," or even assist with "noncombatant services" if asked, because it goes against their particular belief system or religion. If you are one of those people, you are legally allowed to ask for a "Modified Oath of Allegiance." This is something you must request at the time of the interview, if you are not comfortable answering "Yes" to all six questions listed previously. There are three requirements to receive a modified oath:

1. You are opposed to bearing arms or otherwise serving in the armed forces.
2. Your opposition is based on religious principles or a belief system.
3. Your belief is sincere, meaningful, and deeply held.

If you request a modified oath, you may be asked to describe your beliefs or religion during the interview. The interviewer wants to make sure that you are being honest, truthful, and sincere. Be prepared to talk in detail about your beliefs.

Words and Phrases to Know

Constitution: the supreme law of the land
Oath: a promise
Oath of Allegiance: promise to be loyal to the United States
Bear arms: fight for the United States
Noncombatant services: work for the United States, but not fight

Oath of Allegiance

I hereby declare, on oath, that I absolutely and entirely renounce and abjure all allegiance and fidelity to any foreign prince, potentate, state, or sovereignty, of whom or which I have heretofore been a subject or citizen;

that I will support and defend the Constitution and laws of the United States when required by law;

that I will bear true faith and allegiance to the same;

that I will bear arms on behalf of the United States when required by law;

that I will perform noncombatant service in the Armed Forces of the United States when required by law;

that I will perform work of national importance under civilian direction when required by law; and that I take this obligation freely, without any mental reservation or purpose of evasion; so help me God.

10 ▶ LANGUAGE AND KNOWLEDGE ASSESSMENT

During your interview, you will also be asked to show that you can read and write basic English. You will also be tested on basic U.S. history and civics from the 100 questions covered in Section II.

For some candidates, this portion of the citizenship exam can be very stressful. Listening carefully and clearly understanding words can be difficult if English is not your first language. Here are three ways to boost your listening skills, which will help you to hear and understand English.

- **Listen closely and quietly**—to the radio, to the television, and to others that you meet during the course of the day. Try repeating silently to yourself the phrases they say. Notice when you remember a phrase correctly and when you don't.
- **Find role models**—listen carefully to radio and television newscasters, talk show hosts, members of the clergy, and others who are effective speakers. Try writing down a sentence that they say. Did you get it right or wrong?
- **Keep a journal**—include words and phrases that give you trouble. Practice saying them aloud and writing them down.

Active listening is a way of showing a speaker that you really hear what he or she is saying. When you listen actively, you get the information that you need and are able to provide the speaker with valuable feedback.

HOW TO LISTEN ACTIVELY

- Pay attention
- Nod your head up and down at the speaker
- Use verbal confirmation, such as saying, "I see"
- Make eye contact

100 Questions

Your interviewer will ask you **ten** U.S. history and civics questions from the list of 100 questions. You must answer **six** of these questions correctly to pass. Go back and review Section II to study the 100 questions.

You may try to repeat the main idea of the question at the beginning of your answer. This shows the interviewer that you understand the question. Plus, it gives you some time to think while you decide on your answer.

For example, if the interviewer asks, "Name one problem that led to the Civil War?" you could answer, "One problem that led to the Civil War was slavery."

However, don't feel pressured to answer in full sentences. Simply stating, "slavery," is enough for a correct answer! Here is an example of how this portion of the interview could proceed:

Interviewer: Now I'm going to ask you some questions about U.S. history and government.

Q: Which president is called the "father of our country"?
A: _____

Q: What is the Constitution?
A: _____

Q: Who is the vice president of the United States now?
A: _____

Q: There were 13 original states. Name one.
A: _____

Q: What did the Emancipation Proclamation do?
A: _____

Q: Name one state that borders Canada.
A: _____

Q: What major event occurred on September 11, 2001?
A: _____

Q: When do we celebrate Independence Day?
A: _____

Q: Where is the Statue of Liberty located?
A: _____

Q: What is the capital of your state?
A: _____

Writing

The interviewer will read you one sentence from a list of sentences similar to those you have already practiced. He or she will ask you to listen, and then write the sentence down on a blank piece of paper. The interviewer will repeat the sentence to you multiple times. If you are unable to write the sentence correctly, you will be given two other sentences to try and write down correctly. Remember to listen carefully and ask your interviewer to repeat the sentence if you did not hear it well.

> **Interviewer:** Now I want you to write the sentence that I say.
> *Who can vote.*
>
> **What you do:** Write the sentence!
> _____.

Reading

The interviewer will show you a list of three sentences. Beginning with sentence one, he or she will ask you to read it out loud. If you read it correctly, you have passed! If you cannot read sentence one, you will be given a second and third sentence, with different words, to try. Take your time, and sound each word out slowly. As long as you are able to read one of the three sentences, you will pass!

> **Interviewer:** Now I am going to show you a sentence. Please read it out loud.
> *Citizens can vote.*
>
> **What you do:** Read it out loud!

Vocabulary Lists

On the next page is the official USCIS vocabulary list for the reading and writing portions of the U.S. Citizenship Exam. Notice that the content focuses on civics and history. These are the only words that will be tested. The more you study these words, the easier it will be to pass your exam. Practice!

WRITING VOCABULARY

PEOPLE	CIVICS	PLACES
Adams	American Indian	Alaska
Lincoln	capital	California
Washington	citizens	Delaware
American Indian	Civil War	Canada
Congress	congress	Mexico
	Father of Our Country	New York City
	flag	United States
	free	Washington
	freedom of speech	Washington D.C.
	president	
	right	
	senators	
	state/states	
	White House	

MONTHS	HOLIDAYS	VERBS	OTHER (FUNCTION)	OTHER (CONTENT)
February	President's Day	can	and	blue
May	Memorial Day	come	during	dollar bill
June	Flag Day	elect	for	fifty/50
July	Independence Day	have/has	here	first
September	Labor Day	it/was/be	in	largest
October	Columbus Day	lives/lived	of	most
November	Thanksgiving	meets	on	north
		pay	the	one
		vote	to	one hundred/100
		want	we	people
				red
				second
				south
				taxes
				white

READING VOCABULARY

PEOPLE	CIVICS	PLACES	HOLIDAYS
Abraham Lincoln	American Flag	America	President's Day
George Washington	Bill of Rights	United States	Memorial Day
	capital	U.S.	Flag Day
	citizen		Independence Day
	city		Labor Day
	congress		Columbus Day
	country		Thanksgiving
	Father of Our Country		
	government		
	president		
	right		
	senators		
	state/states		
	White House		

QUESTION WORDS	VERBS	OTHER (FUNCTION)	OTHER (CONTENT)
How	can	a	colors
What	come	for	dollar bill
When	do/does	here	first
Where	elects	in	largest
Who	have/has	of	many
Why	is/are/was/be	on	most
	lives/lived	the	north
	meet	to	one
	name	we	people
	pay		second
	vote		south
	want		

SECTION REVIEW ▶

Remember the three useful phrases, and be sure that you can answer all of the following questions. Review this section if you need help.

Useful Phrases

- Please repeat that.
- Please speak more slowly.
- Please speak louder.

Greetings and Small Talk

- How are you?
- What is the weather like today? / How is the weather?
- What did you have for breakfast this morning?
- How did you get here today? / Who came with you?
- What day of the week is today?
- Do you know why you are here today?
- Why do you want to be a U.S. citizen?
- Do you have any questions before we begin?
- Have you studied for the citizenship test? What did you do?

Time Questions

- When did you first come to the United States?
- How long have you been a permanent resident?
- When was your last trip out of the United States?
- How long were you gone?
- How long have you lived at (current address)?
- How long have you worked at (current job)?

Place Questions

- Where did you first enter the United States? / What is your port of entry?
- What is your country of nationality?
- What is your country of birth? / Where were you born?

Have You Ever Questions

- **Have you ever** failed to file a tax return?
- **Have you ever** been part of the communist party / a terrorist organization?
- **Have you ever** been arrested, indicted, or convicted of a crime?

Another way to categorize these questions is by question word. Listen carefully to the first word of each question and the key words in the question. Ask your interviewer to repeat the question if you did not hear it the first time.

"What" Questions

- **What** is your name?
- **What** is your Social Security number?
- **What** is your home telephone number?
- **What** is your date of birth?
- **What** is your marital status?
- **What** is your nationality?
- **What** is your height / weight / eye color / hair color?
- **What** is your address?
- **What** is your husband's / wife's name?
- **What** is his / her immigration status?

"How" Questions

- **How** are you?
- **How** is the weather?
- **How** did you get here?
- **How** do you spell your last name?

"How Long" Questions

- **How long** have you been a permanent resident?
- **How long** have you lived at (current address)?
- **How long** have you worked at (current job)?
- **How long** did the trip outside the United States last?
- **How long** have you been married?

"Where" Questions

- **Where** were you born?
- **Where** do you live?
- **Where** do you work?
- **Where** did you go (when you last left the United States)?
- **Where** were your children born?

"When" Questions

- **When** were you born?
- **When** did you come to the United States?
- **When** did you get your permanent resident card?

- **When** did you get married?
- **When** did your spouse become a citizen?
- **When** did you move to (current address)?
- **When** was your last trip outside the United States?
- **When** did you return?
- **When** were your children born?

"Why" Questions

- **Why** do you want to become a citizen?
- **Why** were you out of the country for six months or longer?
- **Why** did you get divorced?
- **Why** aren't you working?

APPENDIX A
SAMPLE N-400 APPLICATION

This appendix contains a copy of the most current N-400 "Application for Naturalization." You can practice filling it out, but this is not the real application. You can get the real application from an USCIS office near you or online at www.uscis.gov. Remember that USCIS changes the N-400 from time to time, so the one you fill out might look a bit different from the one in this appendix.

Application for Naturalization

Department of Homeland Security

U.S. Citizenship and Immigration Services

USCIS
Form N-400
OMB No. 1615-0052
Expires 03/31/2019

For USCIS Use Only	Date Stamp	Receipt	Action Block

Remarks	

▶ **START HERE - Type or print in black ink.** Type or print "N/A" if an item is not applicable or the answer is none, unless otherwise indicated. Failure to answer all of the questions may delay U.S. Citizenship and Immigration Services (USCIS) processing your Form N-400. **NOTE: You must complete Parts 1. - 15.**

If your biological or legal adoptive mother or father is a U.S. citizen by birth, or was naturalized before you reached your 18th birthday, you may already be a U.S. citizen. Before you consider filing this application, please visit the USCIS Website at www.uscis.gov for more information on this topic and to review the instructions for Form N-600, Application for Certificate of Citizenship, and Form N-600K, Application for Citizenship and Issuance of Certificate Under Section 322.

NOTE: Are either of your parents a United States citizen? If you answer "Yes," then complete **Part 6. Information About Your Parents** as part of this application. If you answer "No," then skip **Part 6.** and go to **Part 7. Biographic Information.**

Part 1. Information About Your Eligibility (Select only one box or your Form N-400 may be delayed)

Enter Your 9 Digit A-Number:
▶ A- [ ][ ][ ][ ][ ][ ][ ][ ][ ]

1. You are at least 18 years of age **and:**

   A. ☐ Have been a lawful permanent resident of the United States for at least 5 years.

   B. ☐ Have been a lawful permanent resident of the United States for at least 3 years. In addition, you have been married to and living with the same U.S. citizen spouse for the last 3 years, **and** your spouse has been a U.S. citizen for the last 3 years at the time you filed your Form N-400.

   C. ☐ Are a lawful permanent resident of the United States **and** you are the spouse of a U.S. citizen **and** your U.S. citizen spouse is regularly engaged in specified employment abroad. (See the Immigration and Nationality Act (INA) section 319(b).) If your residential address is outside the United States and you are filing under Section 319(b), select the USCIS Field Office from the list below where you would like to have your naturalization interview:

   [   ]

   D. ☐ Are applying on the basis of qualifying military service.

   E. ☐ Other (Explain): [   ]

Part 2. Information About You (Person applying for naturalization)

1. Your Current Legal Name (**do not** provide a nickname)

Family Name (Last Name)	Given Name (First Name)	Middle Name (if applicable)

2. Your Name Exactly As It Appears on Your Permanent Resident Card (if applicable)

Family Name (Last Name)	Given Name (First Name)	Middle Name (if applicable)

Part 2. Information About You (Person applying for naturalization) (continued) A- ☐☐☐☐☐☐☐☐☐

3. Other Names You Have Used Since Birth (include nicknames, aliases, and maiden name, if applicable)

Family Name (Last Name)	Given Name (First Name)	Middle Name (if applicable)

4. Name Change (Optional)

   Read the Form N-400 Instructions before you decide whether or not you would like to legally change your name.

   Would you like to legally change your name?　　　　　　　☐ Yes　☐ No

   If you answered "Yes," type or print the new name you would like to use in the spaces provided below.

Family Name (Last Name)	Given Name (First Name)	Middle Name (if applicable)

5. U.S. Social Security Number (if applicable)　　6. USCIS Online Account Number (if any)

   ▶ ☐☐☐☐☐☐☐☐☐　　　　▶ ☐☐☐☐☐☐☐☐☐☐☐☐

7. Gender　　　　8. Date of Birth (mm/dd/yyyy)　　9. Date You Became a Lawful Permanent Resident (mm/dd/yyyy)

   ☐ Male　☐ Female

10. Country of Birth　　　　　　11. Country of Citizenship or Nationality

12. Do you have a physical or developmental disability or mental impairment that prevents you from demonstrating your knowledge and understanding of the English language and/or civics requirements for naturalization?　　☐ Yes　☐ No

    If you answered "Yes," submit a completed Form N-648, Medical Certification for Disability Exceptions, when you file your Form N-400.

13. Exemptions from the English Language Test

    A. Are you **50** years of age or older **and** have you lived in the United States as a lawful permanent resident for periods totaling at least **20** years at the time you file your Form N-400?　　☐ Yes　☐ No

    B. Are you **55** years of age or older **and** have you lived in the United States as a lawful permanent resident for periods totaling at least **15** years at the time you file your Form N-400?　　☐ Yes　☐ No

    C. Are you **65** years of age or older **and** have you lived in the United States as a lawful permanent resident for periods totaling at least **20** years at the time you file your Form N-400? (If you meet this requirement, you will also be given a simplified version of the civics test.)　　☐ Yes　☐ No

Part 3. Accommodations for Individuals With Disabilities and/or Impairments

NOTE: Read the information in the Form N-400 Instructions before completing this part.

1. Are you requesting an accommodation because of your disabilities and/or impairments?　　☐ Yes　☐ No

   If you answered "Yes," select any applicable box.

   A. ☐ I am deaf or hard of hearing and request the following accommodation. (If you are requesting a sign-language interpreter, indicate for which language (for example, American Sign Language).)

   B. ☐ I am blind or have low vision and request the following accommodation:

Part 3. Accommodations for Individuals With Disabilities and/or Impairments (continued)   A-[ ][ ][ ][ ][ ][ ][ ][ ][ ]

C. ☐ I have another type of disability and/or impairment (for example, use a wheelchair). (Describe the nature of your disability and/or impairment and the accommodation you are requesting.)

[   ]

Part 4. Information to Contact You

1. Daytime Telephone Number
[   ]

2. Work Telephone Number (if any)
[   ]

3. Evening Telephone Number
[   ]

4. Mobile Telephone Number (if any)
[   ]

5. Email Address (if any)
[   ]

Part 5. Information About Your Residence

1. Where have you lived during the last five years? Provide your most recent residence and then list every location where you have lived during the last five years. If you need extra space, use additional sheets of paper.

   A. Current Physical Address

     Street Number and Name   Apt. Ste. Flr. Number
     [   ] ☐ ☐ ☐ [   ]

     City or Town   County   State   ZIP Code + 4
     [   ] [   ] [   ] [   ] - [   ]

     Province or Region   Postal Code   Country
     (foreign address only)   (foreign address only)   (foreign address only)
     [   ] [   ] [   ]

     Dates of   From (mm/dd/yyyy)   To (mm/dd/yyyy)
     Residence [   ] [   ]

   B. Current Mailing Address (if different from the address above)

     In Care Of Name (if any)
     [   ]

     Street Number and Name   Apt. Ste. Flr. Number
     [   ] ☐ ☐ ☐ [   ]

     City or Town   County   State   ZIP Code + 4
     [   ] [   ] [   ] [   ] - [   ]

     Province or Region   Postal Code   Country
     (foreign address only)   (foreign address only)   (foreign address only)
     [   ] [   ] [   ]

Part 5. Information About Your Residence (continued)

A- ☐☐☐☐☐☐☐☐☐

C. Physical Address 2

Street Number and Name

[blank]

Apt. ☐ Ste. ☐ Flr. ☐ Number [blank]

City or Town [blank]

County [blank]

State [blank]

ZIP Code + 4 [blank] - [blank]

Province or Region
(foreign address only) [blank]

Postal Code
(foreign address only) [blank]

Country
(foreign address only) [blank]

Dates of Residence   From (mm/dd/yyyy) [blank]   To (mm/dd/yyyy) [blank]

D. Physical Address 3

Street Number and Name

[blank]

Apt. ☐ Ste. ☐ Flr. ☐ Number [blank]

City or Town [blank]

County [blank]

State [blank]

ZIP Code + 4 [blank] - [blank]

Province or Region
(foreign address only) [blank]

Postal Code
(foreign address only) [blank]

Country
(foreign address only) [blank]

Dates of Residence   From (mm/dd/yyyy) [blank]   To (mm/dd/yyyy) [blank]

E. Physical Address 4

Street Number and Name

[blank]

Apt. ☐ Ste. ☐ Flr. ☐ Number [blank]

City or Town [blank]

County [blank]

State [blank]

ZIP Code + 4 [blank] - [blank]

Province or Region
(foreign address only) [blank]

Postal Code
(foreign address only) [blank]

Country
(foreign address only) [blank]

Dates of Residence   From (mm/dd/yyyy) [blank]   To (mm/dd/yyyy) [blank]

Part 6. Information About Your Parents

If neither one of your parents is a United States citizen, then skip this part and go to Part 7.

1. Were your parents married before your 18th birthday? ☐ Yes ☐ No

Information About Your Mother

2. Is your mother a U.S. citizen? ☐ Yes ☐ No

If you answered "Yes," complete the following information. If you answered "No," go to **Item Number 3.**

Part 6. Information About Your Parents (continued)   A- ☐☐☐☐☐☐☐☐☐

A. Current Legal Name of U.S. Citizen Mother

Family Name (Last Name)   Given Name (First Name)   Middle Name (if applicable)

B. Mother's Country of Birth   **C.** Mother's Date of Birth (mm/dd/yyyy)

D. Date Mother Became a U.S. Citizen   **E.** Mother's A-Number
(if known) (mm/dd/yyyy)   (if any)
                                                    ▶ A- ☐☐☐☐☐☐☐☐☐

Information About Your Father

3. Is your father a U.S. citizen?   ☐ Yes   ☐ No

If you answered "Yes," complete the information below. If you answered "No," go to **Part 7.**

A. Current Legal Name of U.S. Citizen Father

Family Name (Last Name)   Given Name (First Name)   Middle Name (if applicable)

B. Father's Country of Birth   **C.** Father's Date of Birth (mm/dd/yyyy)

D. Date Father Became a U.S. Citizen   **E.** Father's A-Number
(if known) (mm/dd/yyyy)   (if any)
                                                    ▶ A- ☐☐☐☐☐☐☐☐☐

Part 7. Biographic Information

NOTE: USCIS requires you to complete the categories below to conduct background checks. (See the Form N-400 Instructions for more information.)

1. Ethnicity (Select **only one** box)
   ☐ Hispanic or Latino   ☐ Not Hispanic or Latino

2. Race (Select **all applicable** boxes)
   ☐ White   ☐ Asian   ☐ Black or   ☐ American Indian   ☐ Native Hawaiian or
                          African American   or Alaska Native   Other Pacific Islander

3. Height   Feet ☐   Inches ☐   **4.** Weight   Pounds ☐☐☐

5. Eye color (Select **only one** box)
   ☐ Black   ☐ Blue   ☐ Brown   ☐ Gray   ☐ Green   ☐ Hazel   ☐ Maroon   ☐ Pink   ☐ Unknown/ Other

6. Hair color (Select **only one** box)
   ☐ Bald   ☐ Black   ☐ Blond   ☐ Brown   ☐ Gray   ☐ Red   ☐ Sandy   ☐ White   ☐ Unknown/
     (No hair)   Other

Part 8. Information About Your Employment and Schools You Attended   A- [ ][ ][ ][ ][ ][ ][ ][ ][ ]

List where you have worked or attended school full time or part time during the last five years. Provide information for the complete time period. Include all military, police, and/or intelligence service. Begin by providing information about your most recent or current employment, studies, or unemployment (if applicable). Provide the locations and dates where you worked, were self-employed, were unemployed, or have studied for the last five years. If you worked for yourself, type or print "self-employed." If you were unemployed, type or print "unemployed." If you need extra space, use additional sheets of paper.

1. Employer or School Name

Street Number and Name   Apt. Ste. Flr. Number
☐ ☐ ☐

City or Town   State   ZIP Code + 4
-

Province or Region   Postal Code   Country
(foreign address only)   (foreign address only)   (foreign address only)

Date From (mm/dd/yyyy)   Date To (mm/dd/yyyy)   Your Occupation

2. Employer or School Name

Street Number and Name   Apt. Ste. Flr. Number
☐ ☐ ☐

City or Town   State   ZIP Code + 4
-

Province or Region   Postal Code   Country
(foreign address only)   (foreign address only)   (foreign address only)

Date From (mm/dd/yyyy)   Date To (mm/dd/yyyy)   Your Occupation

3. Employer or School Name

Street Number and Name   Apt. Ste. Flr. Number
☐ ☐ ☐

City or Town   State   ZIP Code + 4
-

Province or Region   Postal Code   Country
(foreign address only)   (foreign address only)   (foreign address only)

Date From (mm/dd/yyyy)   Date To (mm/dd/yyyy)   Your Occupation

Part 9. Time Outside the United States

A- ☐☐☐☐☐☐☐☐☐

1. How many **total days (24 hours or longer)** did you spend outside the United States during the last 5 years? ☐ days

2. How many trips of **24 hours or longer** have you taken outside the United States during the last 5 years? ☐ trips

3. List below all the trips of **24 hours or longer** that you have taken outside the United States during the last 5 years. Start with your most recent trip and work backwards. If you need extra space, use additional sheets of paper.

Date You Left the United States (mm/dd/yyyy)	Date You Returned to the United States (mm/dd/yyyy)	Did Trip Last 6 Months or More?	Countries to Which You Traveled	Total Days Outside the United States
		☐ Yes ☐ No		
		☐ Yes ☐ No		
		☐ Yes ☐ No		
		☐ Yes ☐ No		
		☐ Yes ☐ No		
		☐ Yes ☐ No		

Part 10. Information About Your Marital History

1. What is your current marital status?

   ☐ Single, Never Married ☐ Married ☐ Divorced ☐ Widowed ☐ Separated ☐ Marriage Annulled

   If you are single and have **never** married, go to **Part 11.**

2. If you are married, is your spouse a current member of the U.S. armed forces? ☐ Yes ☐ No

3. How many times have you been married (including annulled marriages, marriages to other people, and marriages to the same person)? ☐

4. If you are married now, provide the following information about your current spouse.

   A. Current Spouse's Legal Name

Family Name (Last Name)	Given Name (First Name)	Middle Name (if applicable)

   B. Current Spouse's Previous Legal Name

Family Name (Last Name)	Given Name (First Name)	Middle Name (if applicable)

   C. Other Names Used by Current Spouse (include nicknames, aliases, and maiden name, if applicable)

Family Name (Last Name)	Given Name (First Name)	Middle Name (if applicable)

   D. Current Spouse's Date of Birth (mm/dd/yyyy)   E. Date You Entered into Marriage with Current Spouse (mm/dd/yyyy)

   ☐   ☐

Part 10. Information About Your Marital History (continued)   A- ☐☐☐☐☐☐☐☐☐

F. Current Spouse's Present Home Address

Street Number and Name   Apt. Ste. Flr. Number

[   ]   ☐   ☐   ☐   [   ]

City or Town   County   State   ZIP Code + 4

[   ]   [   ]   [   ]   [   ] - [   ]

Province or Region   Postal Code   Country
(foreign address only)   (foreign address only)   (foreign address only)

[   ]   [   ]   [   ]

G. Current Spouse's Current Employer or Company

[   ]

5. Is your current spouse a U.S. citizen?   ☐ Yes   ☐ No

If you answered "Yes," answer **Item Number 6.** If you answered "No," go to **Item Number 7.**

6. If your current spouse is a U.S. citizen, complete the following information.

   A. When did your current spouse become a U.S. citizen?

      ☐ At Birth - Go to **Item Number 8.**   ☐ Other - Complete the following information.

   B. Date Your Current Spouse Became
      a U.S. Citizen (mm/dd/yyyy)

      [   ]

7. If your current spouse is not a U.S. citizen, complete the following information.

   A. Current Spouse's Country of Citizenship or Nationality   **B.** Current Spouse's A-Number (if any)

   [   ]   ▶ A- [   ]

   C. Current Spouse's Immigration Status

      ☐ Lawful Permanent Resident   ☐ Other (Explain): [   ]

8. How many times has your current spouse been married (including annulled marriages, marriages to   [   ]
other people, and marriages to the same person)? If your current spouse has been married before,
provide the following information about your current spouse's prior spouse.

If your current spouse has had more than one previous marriage, provide that information on additional sheets of paper.

   A. Legal Name of My Current Spouse's Prior Spouse

   Family Name (Last Name)   Given Name (First Name)   Middle Name (if applicable)

   [   ]   [   ]   [   ]

   B. Immigration Status of My Current Spouse's Prior Spouse (if known)

      ☐ U.S. Citizen   ☐ Lawful Permanent Resident   ☐ Other (Explain): [   ]

   C. Date of Birth of My Current Spouse's   **D.** Country of Birth of My Current Spouse's
   Prior Spouse (mm/dd/yyyy)   Prior Spouse

   [   ]   [   ]

   E. Country of Citizenship or Nationality of My Current
   Spouse's Prior Spouse

   [   ]

Part 10. Information About Your Marital History (continued) A- ☐☐☐☐☐☐☐☐☐

F. My Current Spouse's Date of Marriage with Prior Spouse (mm/dd/yyyy)

G. Date My Current Spouse's Marriage Ended with Prior Spouse (mm/dd/yyyy)

H. How My Current Spouse's Marriage Ended with Prior Spouse

☐ Annulled ☐ Divorced ☐ Spouse Deceased ☐ Other (Explain):

9. If you were married before, provide the following information about your prior spouse. If you have more than one previous marriage, provide that information on additional sheets of paper.

A. My Prior Spouse's Legal Name

Family Name (Last Name)　　　Given Name (First Name)　　　Middle Name (if applicable)

B. My Prior Spouse's Immigration Status When My Marriage Ended (if known)

☐ U.S. Citizen ☐ Lawful Permanent Resident ☐ Other (Explain):

C. My Prior Spouse's Date of Birth (mm/dd/yyyy)

D. My Prior Spouse's Country of Birth

E. My Prior Spouse's Country of Citizenship or Nationality

F. Date of Marriage with My Prior Spouse (mm/dd/yyyy)

G. Date Marriage Ended with My Prior Spouse (mm/dd/yyyy)

H. How Marriage Ended with My Prior Spouse

☐ Annulled ☐ Divorced ☐ Spouse Deceased ☐ Other (Explain):

Part 11. Information About Your Children

1. Indicate your total number of children. (You must indicate **ALL** children, including: children who are alive, missing, or deceased; children born in the United States or in other countries; children under 18 years of age or older; children who are currently married or unmarried; children living with you or elsewhere; current stepchildren; legally adopted children; **and** children born when you were not married.)

2. Provide the following information about all your children (sons and daughters) listed in **Item Number 1.**, regardless of age. To list any additional children, use additional sheets of paper.

A. Child 1

Current Legal Name

Family Name (Last Name)　　　Given Name (First Name)　　　Middle Name (if applicable)

A-Number (if any)　　　Date of Birth (mm/dd/yyyy)　　Country of Birth

▶ A- ☐☐☐☐☐☐☐☐☐

Part 11. Information About Your Children (continued)	A-									

Current Address

Street Number and Name | Apt. ☐ Ste. ☐ Flr. ☐ Number

City or Town | County | State | ZIP Code + 4 | -

Province or Region
(foreign address only)

Postal Code
(foreign address only)

Country
(foreign address only)

What is your child's relationship to you? (for example, biological child, stepchild, legally adopted child)

B. Child 2

Current Legal Name

Family Name (Last Name) | Given Name (First Name) | Middle Name (if applicable)

A-Number (if any)
► A- | Date of Birth (mm/dd/yyyy) | Country of Birth

Current Address

Street Number and Name | Apt. ☐ Ste. ☐ Flr. ☐ Number

City or Town | County | State | ZIP Code + 4 | -

Province or Region
(foreign address only)

Postal Code
(foreign address only)

Country
(foreign address only)

What is your child's relationship to you? (for example, biological child, stepchild, legally adopted child)

C. Child 3

Current Legal Name

Family Name (Last Name) | Given Name (First Name) | Middle Name (if applicable)

A-Number (if any)
► A- | Date of Birth (mm/dd/yyyy) | Country of Birth

Part 11. Information About Your Children (continued)   A- ☐☐☐☐☐☐☐☐☐

Current Address

Street Number and Name   Apt. Ste. Flr. Number
[_____]   ☐   ☐   ☐   [_____]

City or Town   County   State   ZIP Code + 4
[_____]   [_____]   [_____]   [____] - [____]

Province or Region   Postal Code   Country
(foreign address only)   (foreign address only)   (foreign address only)
[_____]   [_____]   [_____]

What is your child's relationship to you? (for example, biological child,   [_____]
stepchild, legally adopted child)

D. Child 4

Current Legal Name

Family Name (Last Name)   Given Name (First Name)   Middle Name (if applicable)
[_____]   [_____]   [_____]

A-Number (if any)   Date of Birth (mm/dd/yyyy) Country of Birth
▶ A- [_____]   [_____]   [_____]

Current Address

Street Number and Name   Apt. Ste. Flr. Number
[_____]   ☐   ☐   ☐   [_____]

City or Town   County   State   ZIP Code + 4
[_____]   [_____]   [_____]   [____] - [____]

Province or Region   Postal Code   Country
(foreign address only)   (foreign address only)   (foreign address only)
[_____]   [_____]   [_____]

What is your child's relationship to you? (for example, biological child,   [_____]
stepchild, legally adopted child)

Part 12. Additional Information About You (Person Applying for Naturalization)

Answer **Item Numbers 1. - 21.** If you answer "Yes" to any of these questions, include a typed or printed explanation on additional sheets of paper.

1. Have you **EVER** claimed to be a U.S. citizen (in writing or any other way)?   ☐ Yes ☐ No

2. Have you **EVER** registered to vote in any Federal, state, or local election in the United States?   ☐ Yes ☐ No

3. Have you **EVER** voted in any Federal, state, or local election in the United States?   ☐ Yes ☐ No

4. A. Do you now have, or did you **EVER** have, a hereditary title or an order of nobility in any foreign   ☐ Yes ☐ No
      country?

   B. If you answered "Yes," are you willing to give up any inherited titles or orders of nobility that you   ☐ Yes ☐ No
      have in a foreign country at your naturalization ceremony?

5. Have you **EVER** been declared legally incompetent or been confined to a mental institution?   ☐ Yes ☐ No

Part 12. Additional Information About You (Person Applying for Naturalization) (continued)

A- [ ][ ][ ][ ][ ][ ][ ][ ][ ]

6. Do you owe any overdue Federal, state, or local taxes? ☐ Yes ☐ No

7. **A.** Have you **EVER** not filed a Federal, state, or local tax return since you became a lawful permanent resident? ☐ Yes ☐ No

    B. If you answered "Yes," did you consider yourself to be a "non-U.S. resident"? ☐ Yes ☐ No

8. Have you called yourself a "non-U.S. resident" on a Federal, state, or local tax return since you became a lawful permanent resident? ☐ Yes ☐ No

9. **A.** Have you **EVER** been a member of, involved in, or in any way associated with, any organization, association, fund, foundation, party, club, society, or similar group in the United States or in any other location in the world? ☐ Yes ☐ No

    B. If you answered "Yes," provide the information below. If you need extra space, attach the names of the other groups on additional sheets of paper and provide any evidence to support your answers.

Name of the Group	Purpose of the Group	Dates of Membership	
		From (mm/dd/yyyy)	To (mm/dd/yyyy)

10. Have you **EVER** been a member of, or in any way associated (either directly or indirectly) with:

    A. The Communist Party? ☐ Yes ☐ No

    B. Any other totalitarian party? ☐ Yes ☐ No

    C. A terrorist organization? ☐ Yes ☐ No

11. Have you **EVER** advocated (either directly or indirectly) the overthrow of any government by force or violence? ☐ Yes ☐ No

12. Have you **EVER** persecuted (either directly or indirectly) any person because of race, religion, national origin, membership in a particular social group, or political opinion? ☐ Yes ☐ No

13. Between March 23, 1933 and May 8, 1945, did you work for or associate in any way (either directly or indirectly) with:

    A. The Nazi government of Germany? ☐ Yes ☐ No

    B. Any government in any area occupied by, allied with, or established with the help of the Nazi government of Germany? ☐ Yes ☐ No

    C. Any German, Nazi, or S.S. military unit, paramilitary unit, self-defense unit, vigilante unit, citizen unit, police unit, government agency or office, extermination camp, concentration camp, prisoner of war camp, prison, labor camp, or transit camp? ☐ Yes ☐ No

Part 12. Additional Information About You (Person Applying for Naturalization) (continued)

A- ☐☐☐☐☐☐☐☐☐

14. Were you **EVER** involved in any way with any of the following:

    A. Genocide? ☐ Yes ☐ No

    B. Torture? ☐ Yes ☐ No

    C. Killing, or trying to kill, someone? ☐ Yes ☐ No

    D. Badly hurting, or trying to hurt, a person on purpose? ☐ Yes ☐ No

    E. Forcing, or trying to force, someone to have any kind of sexual contact or relations? ☐ Yes ☐ No

    F. Not letting someone practice his or her religion? ☐ Yes ☐ No

15. Were you **EVER** a member of, or did you **EVER** serve in, help, or otherwise participate in, any of the following groups:

    A. Military unit? ☐ Yes ☐ No

    B. Paramilitary unit (a group of people who act like a military group but are not part of the official military)? ☐ Yes ☐ No

    C. Police unit? ☐ Yes ☐ No

    D. Self-defense unit? ☐ Yes ☐ No

    E. Vigilante unit (a group of people who act like the police, but are not part of the official police)? ☐ Yes ☐ No

    F. Rebel group? ☐ Yes ☐ No

    G. Guerrilla group (a group of people who use weapons against or otherwise physically attack the military, police, government, or other people)? ☐ Yes ☐ No

    H. Militia (an army of people, not part of the official military)? ☐ Yes ☐ No

    I. Insurgent organization (a group that uses weapons and fights against a government)? ☐ Yes ☐ No

16. Were you **EVER** a worker, volunteer, or soldier, or did you otherwise **EVER** serve in any of the following:

    A. Prison or jail? ☐ Yes ☐ No

    B. Prison camp? ☐ Yes ☐ No

    C. Detention facility (a place where people are forced to stay)? ☐ Yes ☐ No

    D. Labor camp (a place where people are forced to work)? ☐ Yes ☐ No

    E. Any other place where people were forced to stay? ☐ Yes ☐ No

17. Were you **EVER** a part of any group, or did you **EVER** help any group, unit, or organization that used a weapon against any person, or threatened to do so? ☐ Yes ☐ No

    A. If you answered "Yes," when you were part of this group, or when you helped this group, did you ever use a weapon against another person? ☐ Yes ☐ No

    B. If you answered "Yes," when you were part of this group, or when you helped this group, did you ever tell another person that you would use a weapon against that person? ☐ Yes ☐ No

18. Did you **EVER** sell, give, or provide weapons to any person, or help another person sell, give, or provide weapons to any person? ☐ Yes ☐ No

    A. If you answered "Yes," did you know that this person was going to use the weapons against another person? ☐ Yes ☐ No

    B. If you answered "Yes," did you know that this person was going to sell or give the weapons to someone who was going to use them against another person? ☐ Yes ☐ No

Part 12. Additional Information About You (Person Applying for Naturalization) (continued)

A- ☐☐☐☐☐☐☐☐☐

19. Did you **EVER** receive any type of military, paramilitary (a group of people who act like a military group but are not part of the official military), or weapons training? ☐ Yes ☐ No

20. Did you **EVER** recruit (ask), enlist (sign up), conscript (require), or use any person under 15 years of age to serve in or help an armed force or group? ☐ Yes ☐ No

21. Did you **EVER** use any person under 15 years of age to do anything that helped or supported people in combat? ☐ Yes ☐ No

If any of Item Numbers 22. - 28. apply to you, you must answer "Yes" even if your records have been sealed, expunged, or otherwise cleared. You must disclose this information even if someone, including a judge, law enforcement officer, or attorney, told you that it no longer constitutes a record or told you that you do not have to disclose the information.

22. Have you **EVER** committed, assisted in committing, or attempted to commit, a crime or offense for which you were **NOT** arrested? ☐ Yes ☐ No

23. Have you **EVER** been arrested, cited, or detained by any law enforcement officer (including any immigration official or any official of the U.S. armed forces) for any reason? ☐ Yes ☐ No

24. Have you **EVER** been charged with committing, attempting to commit, or assisting in committing a crime or offense? ☐ Yes ☐ No

25. Have you **EVER** been convicted of a crime or offense? ☐ Yes ☐ No

26. Have you **EVER** been placed in an alternative sentencing or a rehabilitative program (for example, diversion, deferred prosecution, withheld adjudication, deferred adjudication)? ☐ Yes ☐ No

27. **A.** Have you **EVER** received a suspended sentence, been placed on probation, or been paroled? ☐ Yes ☐ No

    B. If you answered "Yes," have you completed the probation or parole? ☐ Yes ☐ No

28. **A.** Have you **EVER** been in jail or prison? ☐ Yes ☐ No

    B. If you answered "Yes," how long were you in jail or prison? Years ☐ Months ☐ Days ☐

29. If you answered "No" to **ALL** questions in **Item Numbers 23. - 28.**, then skip this item and go to **Item Number 30.**

If you answered "Yes" to any question in **Item Numbers 23. - 28.**, then complete this table. If you need extra space, use additional sheets of paper and provide any evidence to support your answers.

Why were you arrested, cited, detained, or charged?	Date arrested, cited, detained, or charged. (mm/dd/yyyy)	Where were you arrested, cited, detained, or charged? (City or Town, State, Country)	Outcome or disposition of the arrest, citation, detention, or charge (no charges filed, charges dismissed, jail, probation, etc.)

Part 12. Additional Information About You (Person Applying for Naturalization) (continued)

A- ☐☐☐☐☐☐☐☐☐

Answer **Item Numbers 30. - 46.** If you answer "Yes" to any of these questions, except **Item Numbers 37.** and **38.**, include a typed or printed explanation on additional sheets of paper and provide any evidence to support your answers.

30. Have you **EVER:**

    A. Been a habitual drunkard? ☐ Yes ☐ No

    B. Been a prostitute, or procured anyone for prostitution? ☐ Yes ☐ No

    C. Sold or smuggled controlled substances, illegal drugs, or narcotics? ☐ Yes ☐ No

    D. Been married to more than one person at the same time? ☐ Yes ☐ No

    E. Married someone in order to obtain an immigration benefit? ☐ Yes ☐ No

    F. Helped anyone to enter, or try to enter, the United States illegally? ☐ Yes ☐ No

    G. Gambled illegally or received income from illegal gambling? ☐ Yes ☐ No

    H. Failed to support your dependents or to pay alimony? ☐ Yes ☐ No

    I. Made any misrepresentation to obtain any public benefit in the United States? ☐ Yes ☐ No

31. Have you **EVER** given any U.S. Government officials **any** information or documentation that was false, fraudulent, or misleading? ☐ Yes ☐ No

32. Have you **EVER** lied to any U.S. Government officials to gain entry or admission into the United States or to gain immigration benefits while in the United States? ☐ Yes ☐ No

33. Have you **EVER** been removed, excluded, or deported from the United States? ☐ Yes ☐ No

34. Have you **EVER** been ordered removed, excluded, or deported from the United States? ☐ Yes ☐ No

35. Have you **EVER** been placed in removal, exclusion, rescission, or deportation proceedings? ☐ Yes ☐ No

36. Are removal, exclusion, rescission, or deportation proceedings (including administratively closed proceedings) **currently** pending against you? ☐ Yes ☐ No

37. Have you **EVER** served in the U.S. armed forces? ☐ Yes ☐ No

38. **A.** Are you **currently** a member of the U.S. armed forces? ☐ Yes ☐ No

    B. If you answered "Yes," are you scheduled to deploy overseas, including to a vessel, within the next three months? (Refer to the **Address Change** section in the Instructions on how to notify USCIS if you learn of your deployment plans after you file your Form N-400.) ☐ Yes ☐ No

    C. If you answered "Yes," are you **currently** stationed overseas? ☐ Yes ☐ No

39. Have you **EVER** been court-martialed, administratively separated, or disciplined, or have you received an other than honorable discharge, while in the U.S. armed forces? ☐ Yes ☐ No

40. Have you **EVER** been discharged from training or service in the U.S. armed forces because you were an alien? ☐ Yes ☐ No

41. Have you **EVER** left the United States to avoid being drafted in the U.S. armed forces? ☐ Yes ☐ No

42. Have you **EVER** applied for any kind of exemption from military service in the U.S. armed forces? ☐ Yes ☐ No

43. Have you **EVER** deserted from the U.S. armed forces? ☐ Yes ☐ No

Part 12. Additional Information About You (Person Applying for Naturalization) (continued)

A- ☐☐☐☐☐☐☐☐☐

44. A. Are you a male who lived in the United States at any time between your 18th and 26th birthdays? (This does not include living in the United States as a lawful nonimmigrant.)   ☐ Yes ☐ No

B. If you answered "Yes," when did you register for the Selective Service? Provide the information below.

Date Registered (mm/dd/yyyy)

☐☐☐☐☐☐

Selective Service Number

☐☐☐☐☐☐☐☐☐☐☐

C. If you answered "Yes," but you **did not register** with the Selective Service System and you are:

1. Still under 26 years of age, you must register before you apply for naturalization, and complete the Selective Service information above; **OR**

2. Now 26 to 31 years of age (29 years of age if you are filing under INA section 319(a)), but you did not register with the Selective Service, you must attach a statement explaining why you did not register, and provide a status information letter from the Selective Service.

Answer **Item Numbers 45. - 50.** If you answer "No" to any of these questions, include a typed or printed explanation on additional sheets of paper and provide any evidence to support your answers.

45. Do you support the Constitution and form of Government of the United States?   ☐ Yes ☐ No

46. Do you understand the full Oath of Allegiance to the United States?   ☐ Yes ☐ No

47. Are you willing to take the full Oath of Allegiance to the United States?   ☐ Yes ☐ No

48. If the law requires it, are you willing to bear arms on behalf of the United States?   ☐ Yes ☐ No

49. If the law requires it, are you willing to perform noncombatant services in the U.S. armed forces?   ☐ Yes ☐ No

50. If the law requires it, are you willing to perform work of national importance under civilian direction?   ☐ Yes ☐ No

Part 13. Applicant's Statement, Certification, and Signature

NOTE: Read the **Penalties** section of the Form N-400 Instructions before completing this part.

Applicant's Statement

NOTE: Select the box for either **Item A.** or **B.** in **Item Number 1.** If applicable, select the box for **Item Number 2.**

1. Applicant's Statement Regarding the Interpreter

A. ☐ I can read and understand English, and I have read and understand every question and instruction on this application and my answer to every question.

B. ☐ The interpreter named in **Part 14.** read to me every question and instruction on this application and my answer to every question in _____ , a language in which I am fluent, and I understood everything.

2. Applicant's Statement Regarding the Preparer

☐ At my request, the preparer named in **Part 15.,** _____ , prepared this application for me based only upon information I provided or authorized.

Part 13. Applicant's Statement, Certification, and Signature (continued)   A- ▢▢▢▢▢▢▢▢▢

Applicant's Certification

Copies of any documents I have submitted are exact photocopies of unaltered, original documents, and I understand that USCIS may require that I submit original documents to USCIS at a later date. Furthermore, I authorize the release of any information from any of my records that USCIS may need to determine my eligibility for the immigration benefit that I seek.

I further authorize release of information contained in this application, in supporting documents, and in my USCIS records to other entities and persons where necessary for the administration and enforcement of U.S. immigration laws.

I understand that USCIS will require me to appear for an appointment to take my biometrics (fingerprints, photograph, and/or signature) and, at that time, I will be required to sign an oath reaffirming that:

1) I reviewed and provided or authorized all of the information in my application;

2) I understood all of the information contained in, and submitted with, my application; and

3) All of this information was complete, true, and correct at the time of filing.

I certify, under penalty of perjury, that I provided or authorized all of the information in my application, I understand all of the information contained in, and submitted with, my application, and that all of this information is complete, true, and correct.

Applicant's Signature

3.   Applicant's Signature

➡ [   ]   Date of Signature (mm/dd/yyyy)

NOTE TO ALL APPLICANTS: If you do not completely fill out this application or fail to submit required documents listed in the Instructions, USCIS may deny your application.

Part 14. Interpreter's Contact Information, Certification, and Signature

Provide the following information about the interpreter.

Interpreter's Full Name

1.   Interpreter's Family Name (Last Name)   Interpreter's Given Name (First Name)

2.   Interpreter's Business or Organization Name (if any)

Interpreter's Mailing Address

3.   Street Number and Name   Apt. Ste. Flr. Number

City or Town   State   ZIP Code + 4

Province   Postal Code   Country

Part 14. Interpreter's Contact Information, Certification, and Signature (continued)

A- [ ][ ][ ][ ][ ][ ][ ][ ][ ]

Interpreter's Contact Information

4. Interpreter's Daytime Telephone Number

5. Interpreter's Mobile Telephone Number (if any)

6. Interpreter's Email Address (if any)

Interpreter's Certification

I certify, under penalty of perjury, that:

I am fluent in English and _____, which is the same language specified in **Part 13., Item B.** in **Item Number 1.**, and I have read to this applicant in the identified language every question and instruction on this application and his or her answer to every question. The applicant informed me that he or she understands every instruction, question and answer on the application, including the **Applicant's Certification** and has verified the accuracy of every answer.

Interpreter's Signature

7. Interpreter's Signature

➡

Date of Signature (mm/dd/yyyy)

Part 15. Contact Information, Declaration, and Signature of the Person Preparing This Application, if Other Than the Applicant

Provide the following information about the preparer.

Preparer's Full Name

1. Preparer's Family Name (Last Name)

   Preparer's Given Name (First Name)

2. Preparer's Business or Organization Name (if any)

Preparer's Mailing Address

3. Street Number and Name

   Apt. ☐ Ste. ☐ Flr. ☐ Number

   City or Town

   State

   ZIP Code + 4 -

   Province

   Postal Code

   Country

Part 15. Contact Information, Declaration, and Signature of the Person Preparing This Application, if Other Than the Applicant (continued)

A- [ ][ ][ ][ ][ ][ ][ ][ ][ ]

Preparer's Contact Information

4. Preparer's Daytime Telephone Number

5. Preparer's Mobile Telephone Number (if any)

6. Preparer's Email Address (if any)

Preparer's Statement

7. **A.** ☐ I am not an attorney or accredited representative but have prepared this application on behalf of the applicant and with the applicant's consent.

B. ☐ I am an attorney or accredited representative and my representation of the applicant in this case ☐ extends ☐ does not extend beyond the preparation of this application.

NOTE: If you are an attorney or accredited representative whose representation extends beyond preparation of this application, you may be obliged to submit a completed Form G-28, Notice of Entry of Appearance as Attorney or Accredited Representative, with this application.

Preparer's Certification

By my signature, I certify, under penalty of perjury, that I prepared this application at the request of the applicant. The applicant then reviewed this completed application and informed me that he or she understands all of the information contained in, and submitted with, his or her application, including the **Applicant's Certification**, and that all of this information is complete, true, and correct. I completed this application based only on information that the applicant provided to me or authorized me to obtain or use.

Preparer's Signature

8. Preparer's Signature

➡️

Date of Signature (mm/dd/yyyy)

> **NOTE: Do not complete Parts 16., 17., or 18. until the USCIS Officer instructs you to do so at the interview.**

Part 16. Signature at Interview

I swear (affirm) and certify under penalty of perjury under the laws of the United States of America that I know that the contents of this Form N-400, Application for Naturalization, subscribed by me, including corrections number 1 through _____, are complete, true, and correct. The evidence submitted by me on numbered pages 1 through _____ are complete, true, and correct.

Subscribed to and sworn to (affirmed) before me

USCIS Officer's Printed Name or Stamp

Date of Signature (mm/dd/yyyy)

Applicant's Signature

USCIS Officer's Signature

Part 17. Renunciation of Foreign Titles

A- ☐☐☐☐☐☐☐☐☐

If you answered "Yes" to **Part 12., Items A.** and **B.** in **Item Number 4.,** then you must affirm the following before a USCIS officer:

I further renounce the title of _____ **which I have heretofore held; or**

(list titles)

I further renounce the order of nobility of _____ **to which I have heretofore belonged.**

(list order of nobility)

Applicant's Printed Name

Applicant's Signature

USCIS Officer's Printed Name

USCIS Officer's Signature

Date of Signature (mm/dd/yyyy)

Part 18. Oath of Allegiance

If your application is approved, you will be scheduled for a public oath ceremony at which time you will be required to take the following Oath of Allegiance immediately prior to becoming a naturalized citizen. By signing below you acknowledge your willingness and ability to take this oath:

I hereby declare on oath, that I absolutely and entirely renounce and abjure all allegiance and fidelity to any foreign prince, potentate, state, or sovereignty, of whom or which I have heretofore been a subject or citizen;

that I will support and defend the Constitution and laws of the United States of America against all enemies, foreign, and domestic;

that I will bear true faith and allegiance to the same;

that I will bear arms on behalf of the United States when required by the law;

that I will perform noncombatant service in the armed forces of the United States when required by the law;

that I will perform work of national importance under civilian direction when required by the law; and

that I take this obligation freely, without any mental reservation or purpose of evasion; so help me God.

Applicant's Printed Name

Family Name (Last Name)

Given Name (First Name)

Middle Name (if applicable)

Applicant's Signature

Date of Signature (mm/dd/yyyy)

APPENDIX B
ONLINE RESOURCES ▶

The Internet can be a valuable learning and research tool. Here is a list of websites that can supplement your studies:

Ben's Guide to U.S. Government for Kids www.bensguide.gpo.gov	**Library of Congress** www.loc.gov
Encyclopedia Britannica Online www.britannica.com	**Our Courts** www.ourcourts.org
History Channel Online www.history.com	**USCIS Online** www.uscis.gov/citizenshiptest
History.org www.ushistory.org	**The White House Online** www.whitehouse.gov
iCivics www.icivics.org	

The following are websites where you can find U.S. citizenship preparation material in foreign languages.

U.S. Citizenship and Immigration Services
https://www.uscis.gov/citizenship/other-languages
- Arabic, Chinese, Korean, Spanish, Tagalog, and Vietnamese resources

Catholic Legal Immigration Network, Inc.
https://cliniclegal.org/resources/translations-citizenship-test
- Albanian, Amharic, Bosnian, Burmese, Cambodian/Khmer, Farsi, French, Gujarati, Hindi, Hmong, Lao, Oromo, Portuguese/Brazilian, Punjabi, Russian Somali, Telegu, Thai, Tigrigna, Urdu

Hebrew Immigrant Aid Society
- http://www.hias.org/citizenship-prep-materials
- Subtitled videos of practice USCIS interviews in the following languages: Arabic, Chinese, Nepali, Russian, Bosnian, Somali, and Vietnamese

NOTES

NOTES

NOTES

NOTES